Ten Assholes and a Curmudgeon

by

Bruce Wayne Workman

DORRANCE PUBLISHING CO
EST. 1920
PITTSBURGH, PENNSYLVANIA 15238

Dorrance Publishing Co
585 Alpha Drive
Pittsburgh, PA 15238
Visit our website at www.dorrancebookstore.com

ISBN: 979-8-88812-436-9
eISBN: 979-8-88812-936-4

This book is dedicated to the following:

Cathy Workman, Amanda Chrysler, Christopher Workman, and anyone else who cannot dissociate themselves from the author.

Acknowledgments

I would like to thank all the members of the Workman family who assisted me with their input, especially when my memory was not what it should be; all those whose research I adapted; and the readers of my blog, *Personal Musings of Bruce Wayne Workman,* for selecting the best of the Assholes of the Week.

Contents

Introduction

Congratulations on purchasing this book. If you like researched commentary about the issues of the day, a skeptical look at sacred institutions, memorials, and pseudo-biographies of despicable people, then you have chosen wisely. Please enjoy!

PART I: Personal

Chapter One: Fear and Loathing in Findlay

(With Apologies to Any Surviving Relatives of Hunter S. Thompson)

One's point of view may change a lot between the ages of seven and sixty-seven. I take exception to Thomas Wolfe's title *You Can't Go Home Again*. You certainly can, and it is not always a good idea. I returned to my birthplace and pre-wonder years after nearly sixty years. At that age, I would have learned that saying "It seemed like a good idea at the time" would be an excuse long rendered unnecessary.

When I lived in Findlay, the local newspaper was called *The Findlay Courier*, which should indicate the political climate. It wasn't until the Nixon/Kennedy election that I realized that Democrats were living there.

I left Findlay, not of my own accord. At the age of seven, going on eight—that's another habit left over from youth. You will never hear me say sixty-eight going on sixty-nine—I didn't have much say on matters such as the location of my father's next job. I left the confines of Findlay to enter the even more confining environs of Auburn, Indiana. Looking back, I am reminded of the scene in *National Lampoon's Vacation* where Cousin Eddie told Dale to show Rusty his worm farm. There was little or nothing for a child to do in Auburn.

Like most rural communities, the political atmosphere in Auburn was conservative. It was not right in the name of the local newspaper, *The Evening Star*. Since the road by the country club was called Morningstar Road, I can now only assume there was a cultish fixation on the planet Venus.

Auburn lacked at most minuscule two entertainment venues I had become accustomed to in Findlay: a movie theater and a public swimming pool. I was a small child for my age and the new kid. The checklist for some crummy few years was complete. When children are this bored, they look for anything to get into trouble, possibly as a revenge plot against parents for making them live in a shithole town or class-C city, as the locals used to insist. Smoking and drinking early were entertainment vehicles, as was (further reminiscent of Dale and Rusty) perfecting masturbation techniques.

I stayed in Auburn and the surrounding area for the next sixteen years and graduated from DeKalb High School with a strong background in anxiety and loneliness. I do not have many fond memories of my time there other than meeting my lifetime best friend, and my future wife and the mother of my children. It was those two who kept me from becoming suicidal. I am sorry; this was supposed to be more lighthearted. Suffice it to say that my time there was never idyllic.

I blew a scholarship to attend any state university in Indiana because I was confused about what I wanted to do and not entirely well mentally. My modus operandi was to choose the path of least resistance. I mixed a year working for the USPS in Fort Wayne with a semester at Indiana University—my stint at the Bloomington campus lasted a month. The post office job was one of only two I acquired independently.

After getting married, I knew I had to get a good job to support the family I was planning. So naturally, when my father moved to Bowling Green, Ohio, with the same company that relocated him to Auburn, I went for a laboratory job there. I stayed there for about a year before moving to Texas to engage in only the second job I had gotten without assistance. At this job, I had the opportunity to educate myself in rubber chemistry. Since I was a child, I have been engaged in a quest for knowledge for its own sake. I took a read-and-experiment approach. I probably couldn't pass an organic chemistry course, then or now, but I learned what ingredients did what in a rubber compound. I became good at it and chose it for my career path. I will not go into any detail on the how and what of rubber compounding because it would be excruciatingly boring to read.

There is an old saying, "Rubber people bounce around." I was no exception. My poor wife, taken from her friends and family at a young age and put into the alien environment of Houston, Texas, could never get wholly acclimated to anything and I "controlled" my angst by drinking in those days—I even spent a night in jail in Downtown Houston. All of this is to say that we moved a lot. I worked in Indiana, Texas, Alabama, Michigan, and Ohio. Our most extended stay was in Michigan, where we settled for twenty-three years before taking my final job in Bellefontaine, Ohio.

I recount this travelogue to provide a little background of my exposure to the political beliefs of colleagues and acquaintances. I made only a handful of friends, possibly due to the paranoia of my youth. I liked people well enough but was always disappointed when it came to getting better acquainted. Whether my expectations were too high, or my anxiety and suspicion drove people away, I don't know.

Growing up in a town with a newspaper with the word "Republican" right in the name and moving to a rural community in Indiana, I was exposed exclusively to Conservative Republican politics. I accepted this as a kid but began having the same nagging doubts I had when sent to Sunday School. The creationism story and the story of the great flood and Noah's ark set off alarm bells in my young inquisitive mind. There were conflicting versions of what happened on which day in Genesis, and by being a member of the TV generation who read encyclopedias I knew many animals and plants were out there. Some had to eat the others to survive.

The story of Noah did not hold muster. I figured out early on that if the Bible couldn't possibly be the word of "God," how could an omnipotent, omniscient, loving God be so full of shit? I went along with it and was even confirmed in the local Lutheran Church. I even attended a strict Church of Christ after I got married. But I never ultimately bought it, and I discovered that many Christians also happened to be assholes. After a while, the kid who used to read encyclopedias couldn't even pretend to believe anymore.

Am I an agnostic or an atheist? An agnostic believes the existence of a divine entity is unknowable, and an atheist just flat out says he doesn't believe. Looking at it more closely, you can see no real difference except the concession to the believer that "I can't disprove it either." I can understand the reluctance to come out as an atheist. It is the equivalent of declaring one's homosexuality in the 1950s or earlier. People don't shriek and run away, but they still view it in a suspicious light, as if you declared yourself to be Satan.

By now, you are probably thinking a couple of things: "Boohoo, you act as if you had it so rough" and "What is the point of all this background?" Well, I am just setting the stage for what may be my life's worst decision, and yes, I do engage in self-pity from time to time. Keep in mind that my earliest relocations were not of my volition.

After I was fired, dismissed, or was a victim of restructuring from my job as a senior chemist at HBD/Thermoid in Bellefontaine, Ohio, I had several choices on how and where I would spend the rest of my life. I had a lovely house in nearby Huntsville, which we were happy with (except for well water with H_2S and having to drive thirty miles to shop). *No*, I thought, *it is a seller's market; I own the house outright, and why shouldn't I take a nice profit and move to a modular home in a pleasant park in my old birth city?* I had some fond memories of Hancock Street in Findlay.

I made a very nice profit on the exchange. I paid cash for my new lodgings and cars, so I had no monthly bills except for utilities. *This is going to be great,* I thought. An important thing to remember when considering returning to the town of your birth—yes, I know some of you never left—is that your perspectives change significantly from childhood to retirement. I was no longer the little guy who liked Ike, believed Kennedy would have a direct line to the Vatican—whatever that was—and generally accepted the political philosophy of the *Republican Courier* and my grandparents.

After the Republican party began going crazy in the mid-sixties, I would now be considered a liberal, Satan-worshipping pedophile who was out to destroy the country by not wanting to beat the shit out of homosexuals. Sadly, Findlay fully endorsed the crazy.

Findlay is a city of about forty thousand people. Suppose it did not serve as headquarters for two corporations. Cooper Tire and Rubber Corporation (now owned by Goodyear) and Marathon Petroleum Company (now owned by U.S. Steel) would be another rural Ohio town. Conservative, religious, and resentful that they are a part of flyover America.

The sole reasons for Marathon's operations in Findlay are that gas was found when drilling a water well near Findlay in 1863, and oil was discovered in the surrounding counties. The sole reason that Marathon is still headquartered there is that U.S. Steel chose not to move it after the acquisition. Today Marathon serves mainly as a fossil fuel polluter and a checkwriter for the Republican party. Findlay's other claim to fame is that Ben Roethlisberger played wide receiver on the high school football team—that's right, the coach thought his son was a better fit at quarterback.

During the Trump/Biden election, Findlay went into full psychosis mode. When questioned, a couple of AR-15-toting militia wannabes intimidated black children and spouted the apparent lie that they were there for the children's protection. The local Democratic party's volunteers were harassed at their booth, at both locations, near the Farmers' Market and in front of the courthouse. The Republicans were so rowdy and noisy—getting truckers to honk for Trump—that they were asked to leave the Farmers' Market. Of course, the bimbo mayor told the Toledo news station that both parties were equally involved. Lying had become the mainstay of the Republican party.

I filled my retirement time by investing and writing, but for little money from either. Since I like to write and have strong opinions, I have sent and replied to several letters to the editor of *The Findlay Courier.* If my letter is published or there is a response, I must rely on others to inform me of the fact. My wife will buy the paper on

Saturday for the ads and coupons. Other than that, I am neither a subscriber nor a reader. I used to be able to access the opinion section for free, but lately they want to pay for a subscription to do that. They did not write the content, but they want you to pay to read it. This policy is in line with general policy since the same applies to nearly all the newspaper content. They have a couple of mediocre staff writers to write investigative pieces about a resident's fifteen minutes of fame or the latest bake sale. Other than that, all the content is from AP or directly from the Republican National Committee.

My opinions do not receive much admiration in the community. I have been called an agent of the devil and smarty pants. Intelligent responses are nonexistent thus far, and it is primarily crazy religious zealotry or playground-level taunting. I wrote another letter this week challenging an organization that wants to do off-campus Bible classes during school hours—welcome to Northwest Ohio, where the only meaningful elections are the Republican primaries.

My wife is afraid of retaliatory action, which is understandable given the violent tendencies of the undereducated Republican youth—including men and women in their fifties and sixties. I should be too, but like Hunter S. Thompson, I am well prepared to defend my house and family.

Next: Lies

Chapter Two: Lies

We all tell them, and we start at an early age; we are just not particularly good at it yet. If George Washington said, "I cannot tell a lie," he was lying. Sometimes lies can be beneficial. Lies that spare the feelings of others or are intended to provide needed encouragement fall into this category. There are other types of falsehoods, and many are not necessarily as innocuous.

Some lies are told without intent to deceive, such as rumors passed without confirmation that later prove false. There are those related to the intent to deceive. There are those told where the speaker is ignorant of the facts and does not know whether they are truthful or not and, in some cases, does not care. There is misinformation, and there is disinformation. The differences between the two are awareness of the truth and intent. Is a lie where the teller does not know that what he has said is false still a lie? You will not get the answer from Merriam-Webster, which defines a lie as:

"1 a: an assertion of something known or believed by the speaker or writer to be untrue with intent to deceive.

b: an untrue or inaccurate statement that may or may not be believed true by the speaker or writer."

By this definition, does the First Amendment protect lies? The U.S. Supreme Court has struggled with this question for years, more often than not defining lies as protected speech. In U.S. v. Alvarez, the court ruled that a lie told intentionally and with the probable intent to deceive was still protected speech. Xavier Alvarez was an incorrigible liar who claimed to have been a Vietnam Veteran, a police officer, a Mexican actress' husband, and a Detroit Red Wings player. SCOTUS was not concerned with these particular fabrications, regardless of the apparent pattern. Alvarez ran into trouble when, as a member of a California water board, he announced at a public meeting that he was a retired Marine and the recipient of the Congressional Medal of Honor. Making this claim violated the Stolen Valor Act of 2005, which prohibited wearing, producing, or selling unauthorized military decorations or medals and made misrepresenting oneself as the recipient of any U.S. military decoration or medal a federal misdemeanor. The majority opinion of SCOTUS asserted that since such a lie did little or no harm, the Stolen Valor Act was unconstitutional. Although Alvarez was absolved of this incident, he remained in jail for fraud convictions resulting from other deceptions he had engaged in. In this and other cases involving deceit or libel, if the court erred it was almost always on the side of protected speech. A common theme among Supreme Court rulings is that falsehoods eventually open discussions to discover the truth.

If misinformation, disinformation, manipulation, self-promotion, aggrandizement, and deceit all fall under the umbrella of lies, then we may need either new terminology or sub-classifications. Most of us can agree that there need to be some restrictions on certain types of speech. Fortunately, we have a lot of recent examples of public lies to choose from. Should statements declaring a pandemic is a hoax and suggesting civil disobedience in response to guidelines from health officials receive the same protection as someone stating that Jack London was the real author of the works of Shakespeare? Of course not; that would be ludicrous. Yet, with the current interpretations of the First Amendment, that might be more plausible than it sounds. During times of relative peace, judges are very protective of freedom of speech. During times of war, not so much. This is when restrictions related to national security are often invoked. Most of us know about "clear and present" danger. Still, fewer know the circumstances upon which Oliver Wendell Holmes Jr. wrote these words in his opinion relating to the case of Schenck v. United States. Charles Schenck was convicted under the Espionage Act of 1917 for writing and distributing letters maintaining that the military draft was a form of involuntary servitude—a definition that seems spot on to me; if it were voluntary service, a draft would be unnecessary—and encouraging young men not to respond to their draft notices. It was not precisely yelling fire in a theater, but most considered it close enough. But since it was WWI and there was a need for bodies, the draft was deemed necessary for national security—wars have put civil rights on the backburner. In the same opinion, Holmes defined "present danger" as imminent peril.

There have been many people yelling fire recently. We can all agree that the verifiable lies relating to the 2020 presidential election, which eventually led to an in-surrection, should not be protected speech. Regulating speech of the above nature would require more than "clear and present danger." Those words must be defined in this context, clearly synonymous with apparent. The present can refer to both time and place and could mean either physically near or imminent. What constitutes danger is, of course, subject to interpretation. None of these terms applied to the issue in Schenck v. United States. It is not clear to me that there was a danger—perhaps people would have viewed the letters as editorials and either agreed or disagreed without taking any actions to circumvent the draft laws. If there was any danger, it wasn't present by any definition of the word I know. The ruling was made in the early 20th century during a world war and, although memorable, clearly is not sufficient for an era with the internet, subjective news sources, and intemperate social media. So, where should we go from here?

We already have laws on the books that penalize some forms of lying—including perjury, false advertising, fraud, and defamation (libel and slander)—but even these are subject to judicial interpretation. In New York Times v. Sullivan 1964, the Supreme Court set a different standard for public figures, overturning lower courts, and making it extremely difficult for a public official or celebrity to win a defamation suit.

First, we need to determine what factors of prevarication are the most important in deciding what should be protected and what should be. Then we need to determine the most appropriate measures for deterrence or punishment.

Should awareness be considered? I am using the term to mean whether the speaker or writer is aware of the untruthfulness of what was being communicated. While this is an important personal consideration, it has no place in a criminal or civil action. There are ways to determine whether something was planned, but this would be an unnecessary and cumbersome process for all but the most egregious offenses. The only person who would know the answer to "Did you know you were lying?" would be the accused. We would expect the defendant to be truthful only about this particular question. It would essentially be like asking someone if they were aware their actions were criminal—the answer would be predicted precisely because it is not verifiable and serves an immediate interest. You and I might care to know if someone is a liar or ill informed, but the law cannot, except in some instances. However, the law must distinguish between liars and confabulators, defined as those with memory disorders who tend to fill in the gaps with fabricated memories. The falsehoods uttered by a confabulator are nearly always harmless, which will be discussed in the succeeding paragraphs.

Intent can be seen as similar to awareness, but significant differences exist. Unlike awareness or cognizance, purpose can be determined without the affirmation of the accused. Intent can be presumed via context and consequences. By the rhetoric and tone used in Trump's speech to the crowd on January 6 and in the months leading up to January, we can assume he was not trying to encourage a peaceful protest. The ensuing riot and the fact that he did not attend as promised tend to confirm this presumption. The intent is essential. If one's goal is to deceive to secure employment, obtain a promotion, or make money, there are already laws and practices to deter and deal with the course. If a person intended to lie to make him or herself seem more valuable to acquaintances, the ramifications are not severe or wide-ranging enough that most of us should care.

We can all agree that some lies do great harm. Harm is the most important factor we should address. Some lies can be beneficial. Let's say a child strikes out three times in a game. Is it better to lie and say, "Your swing looks good; maybe we need to work some more on timing," or tell the truth and say, "You suck at this game"? The reality would be cruel and unnecessary in this case. Other lies can incite violence. We must subdivide severity classifications into likelihood and magnitude in the harm category. Chance goes hand in hand with intent. If a lie is intended to cause damage, it is likely high.

On the other hand, there is reckless negligence, where a falsehood can cause harm regardless of the lack of intent. The magnitude of the injury is critical. Should speech that leads to a violent insurrection where peace officers are injured or lose their lives receive the same protection as false statements that cause only mild offense?

The real peril inherent in lies is that people tend to believe them. Most of the time, we believe what people tell us. This is especially true if the teller is family or a friend. It is part of our nature dating back to when information was passed exclusively in verbal form. If someone told us there was a lion in the area, it was more prudent to believe him than to do eyewitness fact-checking. There is another phenomenon known as truth bias, where people tend to believe what they hear even if it has been discredited. Upon recall, people are more likely to see false statements as accurate, even after they have been informed, they are wrong, and factual statements as false under the same conditions. Of course, there is confirmation bias. We tend to believe what we want to be true. As recent evidence indicates, even a pathological liar can convince many people that he is being truthful. Peer pressure can cause us to doubt what we know to be true. We have all heard of the study where "plants in a group study can cause people to change their minds about which object is largest or smallest." People will believe the group over their "own lying eyes." Social media has compounded the problem.

A study by Soroush Vosoughi, Deb Roy, and Sinan Aral of MIT using fact-checked rumors spread on Twitter found that "falsehood diffused significantly farther, faster, deeper, and more broadly than the truth in all categories of information." This may not be that surprising. Liars can be creative. The fundamental truth can be tedious, but a lie can be as exciting as the lair makes it. Even correcting a lie only sometimes works. Studies have shown that when a correction has been issued for falsehood in print or on social media, most respondents still believe the lie over the truth.

We can agree that there must be some speech restrictions. Shouting "Fire!" in a crowded theater is an excellent example, but it needs to be better defined and go further. Communications have changed significantly since 1791, and the authors could not have foreseen the many methods we now have to transmit speech and reach enormous audiences. Free speech is still one of our most cherished rights. Recent attacks on free speech have largely been instigated by those now claiming to be victims. We have seen how dangerous repetitive lying can be, and it hasn't proven easy. In the past, courts have tended to err on the side of protecting nearly all speech, at least when we are not actively at war. We have seen the necessity for further regulation, and I, along with many others, have laid out factors that should be considered when regulating lies. The question remains, who decides? And herein lies the dilemma. Indeed, not any government agency, even an independent one. Look at the FCC and USPS for an example of how a motivated executive can manipulate an independent agency.

For another example of just how badly such an idea could go, imagine an Orwellian Ministry of Truth run by one of Donald Trump's cronies. Legislatures have become too polarized to be trusted with such an important issue without oversight. Traditionally, the courts have been the final arbitrator in matters regarding the Constitution. Still, recently SCOTUS has become overly partisan, and the majority has become prone to making outrageous decisions or punting complex cases. With the independence of a lifetime appointment also comes a lack of accountability.

We need a truly independent and informed body that can consider all the mitigating and aggravating factors, with the power to direct legislation and influence judicial actions. I am still figuring out how this should be done, but it is worthy of consideration. The threat posed by the members of Congress who spread "the big lie" and instigated the insurrection—yes, it was an insurrection despite recent attempts to deny it—is too immediate and too dangerous to leave for history to judge. There has to be a way to hold these individuals and their ilk accountable now. I know members of the House and Senate are exempt from legal action for statements made in the respective chambers. Still, many of these lies were told on traditional and social media, where no such protections are granted. I want to pose a question to anyone in my audience who might be the recipient of a JD. Should citizens take any legal action against those who have made public statements supporting the lie?

SOURCES

The primary sources have been Wikipedia (various topics) and:

Sunstein, Cass R. *Liars: Falsehoods and Free Speech in an Age of Deception.* Oxford University Press, 2021.

Next: You Might Be an Asshole

Chapter Three: You Might Be an Asshole

I am not referring to the assholes like our weekly award winners. They are in a class of their own. Many everyday people around us display inconsideration and indifference to others that define an asshole. You might even have a few of these qualities. I am listing a few warning signs here. If you find yourself answering yes to the questions below, it may be time to ask someone you trust and admire, "Tell me the truth, am I an asshole?"

Do you drive in the left lane on the freeway even when you are not passing another vehicle? You may be an asshole. Major league assholes have gone from Detroit to Disney World, only leaving the left lane to exit.

Do you constantly interrupt others when talking? You may be an asshole. In case you were wondering, the annoyed looks you see on the faces of others are for you.

Do you honk when you drive by the house of someone you know? You may be an asshole. Do you think they rush to the window whenever they hear a horn? It is annoying and without purpose.

Ditto if you honk at someone who has passed you in a car going the other way. The person you recognize will not turn his head on a pivot like a ventriloquist's dummy. More likely, the driver in front of you wonders what the fuck you want.

Do you act like public streets and parking lots are your personal trash bin? You are most likely an asshole.

Do you drive like you have the deed to the highway in your glovebox and other drivers are just nuisances on your road? You may be an asshole.

Do you vote for a straight Republican ticket? You probably are an asshole.

Do you shout "Get a job!" at homeless people? You may be an asshole. Lack of compassion is one of the defining traits.

Do you ask people to admire your abs? You are definitely an asshole.

Do you sit on your motorcycle and unnecessarily rev the engine repeatedly? You are likely an asshole.

Do you ride your motorcycle through residential neighborhoods at night? You guessed it; you are an asshole. The exact diagnosis applies to vehicles with special mufflers that allow you to share the rumble with sleeping neighbors.

Do you urge children to pull your finger and fart when they do so? You are an asshole, and the children know it.

Do you report black people in your neighborhood as suspicious? You are a racist asshole.

PART II: POLITICS

Chapter Four: On Inflation

Inflation may be an old issue by the time this is published, but I doubt it, and if so it will be back. I have a firm belief that most people are stupid and lazy. Like life in the corporate world, assigning blame is much more important than finding solutions. There is very little that a president or the Executive branch can do about the economy or inflation in general. The Federal Reserve Board is independent, and beyond appointing members there is little a president can do. The Federal Reserve tries to control the amount of money in the economy by raising or lowering interest rates to discourage or encourage borrowing and lending. That is the actual extent. As I said, people are stupid and believe a change in leadership will control inflation.

The problem arises when the stupid discover that the new leadership can do no more than the previous one could. This cycle continues every time there is a glitch in the economy. The truth is that the money supply is only one factor in inflation and the economy's health. I assume that my readers are among the intellectual giants—I cite that you purchased this book as evidence that you are not part of Obtuse America. As such, my remarks on the intelligence of American votes are not directed at you.

I am not going into how much better education was in the old days because some of the stupidest people are my age or older, for example, The Villages, FL. I am concerned about the efforts to whitewash U.S. History, ban books, and allow religious instruction in schools, but that is for another essay. I am reminded of the FTX Exchange commercial with Larry David at the signing of the Constitution. When informed of the intention of letting people vote, he exclaims, "What, even the stupid ones?" and, upon receiving an affirmative reply, tries to tear up the Constitution. Such are my feelings about those whose current economic condition is the sole factor in their voting behavior.

But, back to inflation. The economy generally does not move that quickly. Even events like Black Friday or Black Monday are months or years in the making. Inflation works the same way; it takes at least months for the economy to respond to inflationary pressures. Sorry, MAGA fans, most of these inflationary factors and policies were from your boy's watch.

Typically, the supply of goods and the demand for those goods are what determine prices. There are exceptions like price gouging, but these usually occur during other inflationary events. Tariffs are another inflationary factor; they raise prices via taxation. Who do we know was a big fan of tariffs as the nation's chief executive? You only get one guess.

Disruptions in the supply chain are some of the significant inflationary factors. Situations where manufacturers and shippers close for a period, during a global pandemic, for example, cause an inflationary period where supply cannot meet demand. Whether we like to admit it or not, many of our manufactured goods come from China, where the COVID outbreak first hit and resulted in the closure of most manufacturing.

Disruption of manufacturing was only part of the story. Longshoremen could or would not work, so the shipping of goods by sea came to a near standstill. We can remember the hundreds or even thousands of ships waiting for months at sea to be unloaded.

There was also some price gouging or attempts to profit off perceived shortages. Do you remember the people buying toilet paper by the truckload so they could sell it for a profit? Some forgot the necessity of a retail license while local governments did not, and others were betting on a shortage that never occurred. They tried to return the massive amounts they had accumulated but were told there were no returns on toilet paper. I mean, who has ever attempted to return toilet paper? What do you say? "I am giving up shitting or wiping my ass"? I would have added, "Eat lots of prunes and stool softeners; you are going to need to shit a lot if you don't want to rent a storage unit."

Natural events can also cause supply shortages. Whether or not you believe we are in a period of climate change or debate the causes, we have experienced many droughts at various locations within the last few years. Droughts cost crops to fail, or more resources must be used to save them, leading to food shortages. Grocery prices must increase because grocers operate on small margins and must pass on increases. Employing a shaman would serve people who seek quick solutions and adopt a "throw the bums out" voting strategy.

Immigration policies can also contribute to inflation. Whether we agree with morality or not, much of our food supply relies on migrant labor. Large farms rely on cheap migrant labor to run the farms and get the crops to market. More restrictive immigration policies disrupt the labor force for these farms. A "they take our jobs" is a poor excuse for adopting harsh immigration policies; no, they are not rapists and criminals. Many come as a family to work for wages and at jobs that no citizen would take. Whom do we know that made a big issue out of immigration and attempted to wall off our southern border?

The supply and demand for energy play a big part in inflation, as do price-fixing cartels. Our continued reliance on fossil fuels enables exporting countries to price gouge whenever they want by controlling the supply. If we continue to rely so much on traditional fossil fuels and the environmentally detrimental methods of securing local sources, we are at the mercy of OPEC. Allowing energy to be sold as a commodity is also a terrible idea that we support to this day. There are two areas where capitalist greed does not fit in with our society, and this is one. The other is medicine.

Deficit spending can also fuel inflation. When the deficit is large, we have less flexibility on what interest rates to accept. Paying high interest rates does nothing good for the nation. Historically tax cuts and defense spending have contributed more to the deficit than spending on infrastructure and social programs. Whom do we know who institutes massive tax cuts—mainly for those who don't need them—proposes enormous increases in the defense budget and ever aspires to destroy programs on which average Americans rely?

So, my final appeal to Obtuse America is, quit being so stupid! Read something more informative than a Tweet occasionally! Quit being so lazy. Do a little research before forming a set opinion. And don't form inalterable opinions. New information requires rethinking. Also, avoid joining groups at the drop of a hat!

Next: The Threat

Chapter Five: The Threat

We are facing an existential threat to our democratic republic. Others might say "our democracy," but actual democracies are small and exceedingly rare. What we have is a republic based on representative democracy. We do not vote on every action or piece of legislation. Instead, we elect representatives—hypothetically, anyway—to take care of our business.

The prime architect of the threat is Donald J. Trump—whether natural or a horrendous nightmare. His motivations are more a result of malignant narcissism than any political beliefs. The most dangerous aspect of the former president is his ability to build a cult that seems to believe anything he says and will do whatever he commands. It is his followers that pose the greatest peril. They will not only act in the manner he wants but will also vote for or against candidates per his instructions.

These cultists represent a large enough bloc, so the Republicans both fear and rely on them. Fear is not the only reason the disgraced, twice-impeached, and demented ex-president still leads a dysfunctional Republican party. Not all of his followers are from the "basket of deplorables," but a significant number are. There are wannabe paramilitary groups—who prefer to call themselves militias—white supremacists, neo-Nazis, conspiracy nuts—see QAnon—gun-toting morons, and people suffering from malaise for which they are confident the government or anyone other than themselves is at fault. A few also display occasional signs of sanity and might be the hardest nuts to crack.

What causes someone to believe a pathological liar over any reliable source? How can someone believe God sent a misogynist and serial philanderer? Why would anyone think that a satanic cult of vampires with children as targets is running everything and even more incredible that Trump was the noble hero who would end it all? Couldn't we ask similar questions about any cult?

Trump represents the political division of the "As Seen on TV" brand. Only those unfamiliar with his past could buy into the "billionaire business mogul" façade. I have never understood what magically makes something legitimate merely by appearing on television, whether it be a gadget or a pseudo-celebrity. Other than his "reality" TV—the actual reality is unscripted—appeal, he had a couple of other cons that allowed him to gain a cult following. He could convince many people that none of their problems were of their own making, not a hard sell if you think about it—and he persuaded them that he cared about them. The first assertion is never entirely trustworthy, and the second is a blatant lie. Donald Trump does not care about you, me, or anyone other than himself.

DJT is also not an intelligent man. He doesn't want to show his tax returns or his 1 – 12 grades and college transcripts, and there he has his reasons. As far as taxes are concerned, there are two significant reasons: 1. He has often grossly inflated his total wealth figures. 2. A thorough examination of his taxes could show the tax dodges he employed and might lead to criminal charges. As for his grades, by accounts from teachers, family, and classmates, he did not have the excellent academic record he claimed.

What is the point of all of this? He did not possess the means or intelligence to become or accomplish anything as President of the United States. There were always people, both in front and behind the scenes, who took care of business, and it may be there that the most peril lies. We have a former Army general and head of national security who promotes crazy QAnon conspiracies. Trump had top advisers with ties to neo-Nazi and white supremacist organizations who actively support racist laws and rhetoric. These are the men and women behind the myth, and they are the plotters and planners. January 6 will not be the last violent attack on our democracy. We must do everything now to secure voting rights. We have seen that most of the GOP lacks a spine and cannot be relied upon to defend anything. If they return to power, I believe this will be the last decade of the United States of America as a democratic republic.

Next: The Three Classes of Republicans

Chapter Six: The Three Classes of Republicans

I was born into a Republican family in Findlay, Ohio, when the local newspaper was called *The Republican Courier*. My maternal grandfather, my maternal grandmother (who was also anti-Catholic), my father, and my mother were all Republicans. I was unaware there were any Democrats in Findlay until the election of 1960, when some of the kids in the Lincoln School playground shouted slogans favoring John F. Kennedy. My grandparents and my parents were also good, patriotic people—aside from my grandmother's theological bias and the racism that I assume to be a quality shared by nearly all the white residents of Findlay. It is important to remember that racism was never a disqualifying trait in the "Party of Lincoln," even before the Civil and Voting Rights Acts of 1964 and 1965.

I, too, was a Republican and a racist until I learned more about our nation's history and the history of both. Though there was an attempt by Indiana—and I suspect by many other states—to sugarcoat the reason for the Civil War. The firing on Fort Sumter started the war, is what we were told, which I guess is technically accurate. The history teacher said if it was the secession of the southern states, again technically correct, but the reason for these actions was not emphasized. I assume many others could put it all together on their own. What was the Missouri Compromise, and why was it made? Why did the Compromise of 1850 include the Fugitive Slave law? What was the issue behind all of these compromises? The answer to these questions related to owning human beings the same way as owning a horse or a cow. Of course, enslavers did not view the matter this way. To be a participant in this inhumane act had to involve dehumanizing those who had their origins in Africa. This practice continued even after the abandonment of the institution of slavery.

My first vote, as an 18-year-old, was in a primary election, where I voted against Richard Nixon and other Republicans that I thought had the best chance of winning a general election. In those days, one was not required to register a party in the primaries—a fact that irritated a Republican poll worker when I boldly stated my intentions. My first vote in a general election included a vote for George McGovern, one of the few votes he received in Hamilton, Indiana.

With all of this prologue, I intended to convey that despite my conversion to the Democratic party, I have been friends with and respected members of the other party. We could have discussions and arguments about differing political beliefs that were no more animated than a disagreement over whether we liked apples or oranges the most. I acknowledged that there needed to be a counterpart to the Democrats. One-party governments were authoritarian by design. The communist party was the only party in the Soviet Union, mainland China, and Cuba—these were also the times when the vast majority of Republicans acknowledged that a liberal Democrat was not the same as a communist or socialist. It was a time of common decency in discourse. Sure, there were arguments, some quite intense, and attempts to block or undo legislation, but the craziness had not yet begun. We had a few demagogues, George Wallace and Strom Thurmond, to name two, but they were part of the racist nature of the former confederate states and not the rule in either party.

There is some debate about when the Republican Party went off the rails. Some would say it started with Nixon's "southern strategy," but Nixon was just another politician who coveted power above all else. There were still good Republicans left—all one needs to do is witness the Watergate hearings to know that. Others may say Reagan started it, but he was the ultra-conservative of the time. He could and would still compromise for what he believed was the good of the nation. I firmly believe that it started when Mitch McConnell realized his dream to lead the Senate. Mitch was a man without a discernable political philosophy—I think his choice to become a Republican was only due to the political expediency it offered in Kentucky. McConnell craved power for power's sake, and his every move was to preserve or enhance his political power.

The nomination and election of Donald Trump brought the Republican party to complete insanity. Trump was another Republican whose only political viewpoints were to enrich himself and feed his narcissistic need for recognition and power. Portraying himself as a populist—as all demagogues do—he did not give a single shit about the citizens of the United States or the world.

I will address the theme of this article, the three classes of current Republicans now; I had hoped that some Republicans would have the courage to stand up to an apparent narcissistic sociopath. Some did, but only a few were in any position to put a check on his executive power. I was disappointed by a few of the cowards who had formerly shown brief flashes of character.

The first class of Republicans is the ultra-rich narcissists similar to Trump himself—the chief difference being that I am not convinced that Trump is as wealthy as he claims and is not among the 1%. These soulless sociopaths think income inequality is desirable. They seem to sincerely believe they should be able to make as much money as possible and pay comparatively little in taxes. The wealth becomes multigenerational, and many of the current 1% did little or nothing to earn their mind-boggling riches. If the 1% paid what the tax codes, without the loopholes, call for, we could rebuild our infrastructure, ensure affordable healthcare, and fully fund our children's education. Yes, they control that much money! If they only cared one iota about those in the 99%, the U.S. could be a much better place.

The second class of Republicans is "The Racists." This class includes those who have become so accustomed to white privilege that they believe a God-given right has been taken away from them. I am not saying there is no overlap with the other classes or that there aren't some racists who aren't Republicans. But they are a vast group—almost infinitely more significant than the ultra-wealthy—and were recruited by and still encouraged by Trump. These people were formerly forced into the shadows and not accepted by any political party except for the American Nazi Party. Unlike the Nazi Party, many hide under names like the Proud Boys. They are present at Black Lives Matter rallies and protests and were very much at the January 6 insurrection. They would prefer an authoritarian government that persecutes immigrants, those whose skin is not as light as their own, those whose religion is not to their liking, and those whose upper eyelid is of a different shape than theirs. In short, the Republican party has entirely accepted these dangerous assholes into its fold.

The third class could be called "The Idiots." These people are gullible enough to be convinced of the most outlandish claims. This group proves that idiocy can be acquired as well as genetic. They don't understand science or how the scientific method works, so they dismiss it. Instead, many will rally around outlandish religious proclamations as if the theocrats are the ultimate authority. They trust narcissist sociopaths as personal friends, even if said narcissist's fabrications have been repeatedly revealed. They are willing to believe the cryptic nonsense of an anonymous "insider" whose prophecies never come to pass. They form their beliefs in an information vacuum and seek sources confirming them. The Idiots include anti-vaxxers, QAnon followers, right-wing Christians, ignoramuses (usually rural, but some urban), and the outright stupid (Northwest Ohio is well represented in this category). Again, there is an overlap in the other classes.

There is no way home for the conservatives with a conscience, like Liz Cheney and Adam Kinzinger. The party that Mitch McConnell tainted has now gone thoroughly rotten. For any Republicans reading this (fat chance), here is a quick hypothetical syllogism for you. If your party fully accepts you without tension, your conscience is dead, and you are irredeemably evil.

Part III: Real History

Chapter Seven: The Floundering Fathers: Part One

Quick, what do old-time religion and conservative politics have in common? The most obvious answer is the reliance on mythological interpretations. Much like you can "prove" anything with the Bible or equivalent religious text, you can make any point by portraying the founding fathers as a group of men of unimpeachable virtue and collective wisdom. We do not need less accurate U.S. History taught; we need much more. Our general public's lack of understanding and misinformation about this country's history is astounding and discouraging. The general knowledge of early history is comparable to our version of the western frontier in the 19th century via western television shows. Much of the popular accounts of those times come from works of fiction called "dime novels" and are sensationalized tales of events that never happened that way.

The conservative originalist understanding of the period before and after the revolution is not much more accurate. Those trying to build a nation or confederacy of states after rejecting rule by a monarchy, although Britain was and remained a constitutional monarchy, the monarch had more power at that time, especially over colonies. The chief complaint leading to the revolt was the lack of control given to colonists in deciding their fate. Money was an even more significant factor in the form of taxes, but the standard narrative is different. No, we portrayed our younger selves as virtuous folk struggling to be free to unleash our view of paradise on earth. As usual, it was more complex and ignoble; human emotions played a significant role.

Myth #1: The founders wanted the U.S. to be a Christian nation.

This one is so far off the mark that it deserves top mention. Nobody, except for someone who believes: First, an invisible being created everything and constantly monitors its work. Second, the age of the earth is measured in thousands of years, and the universe is less than a week older. Third, a woman who never had sexual relations with a man gave birth to a messiah. Next, a Jewish zombie will return to save all who believe in him and have been doused with magical water. Only someone who holds these beliefs could look at history and come to this conclusion. Yes, it is a fact that some of our first non-Scandinavian settlers arrived to escape religious persecution. Still, there were other places they could go to do that. There is another reason these people came here. Nobody liked them, and they weren't doing well socially or economically in Devon. Of course, this happened a century and a half before the country's founding and reflected nothing of the mindset of the nation's founders.

Why stop at Christian? Why not claim this is an Anglican nation and make the church Henry VIII created to get a divorce the official state church? England's history is full of religious strife, with various kings and queens declaring which particular sect was the correct one at the time. Under the guise of religious preferences, wars were fought, plots hatched, usurpations attempted (sometimes successfully), and homicides committed. The founding fathers did NOT want this for the new nation. They created specific provisions to ensure that there was no state religion. These statements have been printed and are readily available to any literate person. Are you still waiting to be a believer? Let's look at some direct quotes from the founding fathers themselves:

Thomas Jefferson (from a review of legal cases and a letter to Joseph Priestly):
"Christianity neither is nor ever was a part of the common law."
"...this was the real ground of all the attacks on you: those who live by mystery & charlatanerie, fearing you would render them useless by simplifying **the Christian philosophy, the most sublime & benevolent, but most perverted system that ever shone on man,** endeavored to crush your well earnt, & well deserved fame."

John Adams (in *The Treaty of Peace and Friendship*, 1796):
"As the government of the United States of America is not in any sense founded on the Christian Religion,—as it has in itself no character of enmity against the laws, religion or tranquility of Musselmen,—and as the said States never have entered into any war or act of hostility against any Mehomitan nation, it is declared by the parties that no pretext arising from religious opinions shall ever produce an interruption of the harmony existing between the two countries."

Thomas Paine (in *The Age of Reason*):

"Whenever we read the obscene stories, the voluptuous debaucheries, the cruel and tortuous executions, the unrelenting vindictiveness with which more than half the Bible is filled, it would be more consistent than we called it the word of a demon than the word of God. It has served to corrupt and brutalize mankind."

James Madison (letter to Edward Livingston, 1822):

"Notwithstanding the general progress made within the two last Centuries in favor of this branch of liberty, and the full establishment of it, in some parts of our country, there remains in others, a strong bias towards the old error, that without some sort of alliance or coalition between Government & Religion, neither can be duly supported. Such indeed is the tendency to such a Coalition, and such its corrupting influence on both the parties, that the danger can not be too carefully guarded against. And in a Government of opinion, like ours, the only effectual guard must be found in the soundness & stability of the general opinion on the subject. Every new & successful example therefore of a perfect separation between ecclesiastical & Civil matters is of importance. **And I have no doubt that every new example will succeed, as every past one has done, in shewing that Religion & Govt. will both exist in greater purity, the less they are mixed together.** It was the belief of all Sects at one time that the establishment of religion by law was right & necessary; that the true religion ought to be established in exclusion of all others; and that the only question to be decided was, which was the true religion. The example of Holland proved that a toleration of Sects dissenting from the established sect, was safe and even useful. The example of the Colonies now States, which rejected Religious establishments altogether, proved that all Sects might be safely & advantageously put on a footing of equal & entire freedom. And a continuance of their example since the Declaration of Independence has shewn that its success in Colonies was not to be ascribed to their connection with the parent Country. If a further confirmation of the truth could be wanted, it is to be found in the examples furnished by the States which have abolished their religious Establishments. I can not speak particularly of any of the cases except that of Virginia, where it is impossible to deny that religion prevails with more zeal, and a more exemplary priesthood, than it ever did when established and patronized by Public authority. We are teaching the World the great truth, that Governments do better without Kings & Nobles than with them. **The merit will be doubled by the other lesson, that religion flourishes in greater purity, without than with the aid of Government.**"

So there you have it. It is plain that the founding fathers never declared or inferred that this would be a Christian nation. That people still insist on claiming the country was founded with the intent of being anything remotely resembling a theocracy should be cause for alarm. Instead, it is the norm. This phenomenon precedes the Trump post-truth era and is as much a characteristic of the Republican party as it is the Christian right. It has become a central part of their playbook. Set a goal and use any means to achieve it.

Self-interest is the theme here. We are all pro-choice and pro-life when it comes to ourselves. I want to live, and I want to make choices for myself. The difference and the problems come with the desire to make choices for others. If there is one thing Christians and Republicans love more than anything else, it is controlling the behavior of others. A system of belief that wants to control what others can do with their bodies has no claim to liberty or freedom. We are all interested in ourselves and our welfare; the key is how we interact with others—compassion and empathy set apart the major political parties in the United States. Sure, we all think about and care for ourselves, but some can consider others. Although a central tenet of Christianity, it is lacking in most of its adherents. Altruism is rare on the left side of the political spectrum, but it is entirely absent on the right. In short, Democrats care about the welfare of others, and Republicans don't give a shit.

Next: The Floundering Fathers: Part Two

Chapter Eight: The Floundering Fathers: Part Two

When we last left our heroes, they were commenting on the role of religion in the developing nation. The idea that the United States of America was founded on the principles of Christianity and designed to be a Christian nation is misguided. The feedback from the founders suggests a resounding answer of "no way." Mostly, they were decent men, had a basic understanding of human rights, and understood the primary rules of social interaction (treat others the way you would like to be treated). I don't call this the golden rule because that implies it was a Jesus original. Humans had been dealing with each other for nearly a million years before Jesus. If there were any predisposition toward any dogma, it would be more toward humanism than any single religion.

Myth #2: The overriding concern of the founders in establishing the tenets of the Constitution was the welfare of the ordinary person.

Without exception, the founders were members of the elite class of the latter 18th century. The individual who was nearest to having a typical pedigree was the bastard from the West Indies, Alexander Hamilton. Ironically, his political beliefs revealed him to be the biggest snob of the lot.

What some of the more dense citizens tend to forget is that the forerunner to the United States was a series of land grants given by the British monarchy. Each of the original colonies was a boon granted to an individual favored by the king. The colonies were founded and maintained for the benefit of the elite. Those who came here yearning to be free were either out of options in their homelands or sorely disappointed by the promises of being able to control their destinies. States originated from colonies and the interests of their elite rulers. Those whom today sing the praises of states' rights are merely celebrating the Faustian bargains made to establish a republic on the North American continent.

The early colonies were a diverse group of special interests who were chiefly concerned with maintaining those interests. No grandiose sense of individual liberty was involved except the freedom of the elite to pursue their self-interests.

The Articles of Confederation and, later, the Constitution of the United States were nothing more than a series of compromises intended to form a national coalition of the former colonies. The southern colonies were agrarian and labor-intensive, while the northern colonies were more focused on trade and manufacturing. The southern elites had no desire to do the intensive labor themselves or spend their wealth hiring others to do the work, so the plantation owners established the institution of slavery early on.

Of the 64 men regarded as the founding fathers, 49 owned slaves, including four of the first five presidents. The irony of declaring all men created equal while owning humans was not wholly lost on Thomas Jefferson, but he was pragmatic and adept at the required moral gymnastics.

When George III proclaimed that the lands beyond the Appalachian Mountains belonged to the indigenous population and were off limits to those of European descent, many of the founders were busy securing prime real estate through agents and in secrecy. George Washington acquired much land near the Ohio Valley in this manner.

James Madison did much of the writing of the Constitution, but he never intended it to be a permanent fixture. He and Jefferson agreed it would need several revisions as the nation matured. Alexander Hamilton proposed that the president and senators be lifetime appointments from among the educated elite. He withdrew the proposal knowing it would not even get out of his New York delegation.

There is no record of any founders espousing the selection of ordinary men to positions of responsibility. Most colonists were illiterate and trained only as apprentices in specific trades. The founders had no intention of handing over power to them. The great unwashed only have rights today due to compromises made to secure ratification of nine of the thirteen colonies and the additional concessions necessary to obtain unanimity.

Next: The Floundering Fathers: Part Three

Chapter Nine: The Floundering Fathers: Part Three

By naming this series "The Floundering Fathers," there is no intention to disparage the men who took upon themselves the founding of the United States of America. I only meant to convey that they were fallible human beings operating in a challenging political environment. Getting the former colonies to ratify a document establishing a central government was no walk in the park. James Madison was purposely vague, so the courts could interpret the Constitution to suit the times. As near as can be told, none of the founders, including Madison, were clairvoyant. They could not foresee the changes that would occur over the following 233 years. These reasons provide the argument that the originalists make little sense.

First, let's look at the text of the Second Amendment:

"A well regulated Militia, being necessary to the security of a free State, the right of the people to keep and bear Arms, shall not be infringed." [4]

Let's look at that. It does not flow off the tongue and is hard to read or understand. These four sentence fragments need to be clarified when put together as a complete sentence. The Constitution was not Madison's best literary work.

The Bill of Rights was established to address objections to the Constitution. People had recently experienced a centralized, although foreign, oppressive rule that was suspicious of a new central government. Under the Articles of Confederation, the central government was essentially powerless, and the Article became unworkable. The Constitution was the remedy to states going their ways with no federal government, and the Bill of Rights was created to appease resistant factions. Madison received much criticism from both sides when he published the twelve amendments, presented initially as the Bill of Rights. Note: The English crafted a Bill of Rights earlier.

The idea that the founders were of one mind is ludicrous. Even a cursory examination of the writings of the individuals who attended the Constitutional Convention (no one from Rhode Island attended) shows major disagreements between all involved. Since none of us can read minds (pay no attention to the charlatans who claim they can, it is a trick) and especially cannot read the minds of people who have been dead for two hundred years, we must rely on what they wrote to gain an understanding of their thoughts.

There were two camps: the Federalists, who wanted or at least saw the need for a strong central government, and the anti-Federalists, who thought a weak central government and strong state governments were more desirable. One element upon which they agreed was a distaste for a standing army. They had just experienced a foreign one quartering in their homes and surveilling them and had a severe distrust of armies. The difference was that the Federalists remembered the poor performance of the militias during the revolution and saw the need for a standing army with a powerful navy (they were aware of the barrier an ocean provided).

The need for an armed force was an important debate to remember when analyzing the Second Amendment's meaning and is central to its creation. Thus, the anti-Federalists and others opposed to a federal standing arm were appeased. As James P. Campbell wrote, "James Madison introduced the Second Amendment to placate various fears regarding the military, the balance of power between the federal and state governments, and the use of standing armies." [1]

Had the anti-Federalists and later originalists had their way, there would be no U.S. Army, Marines, Air Force, or Space Force (they could not have imagined the latter two). Our only military would be a navy, which includes coast guard duties and fifty in-dependent state militias or National Guard units. The Federalists recalled the performance of the militias during the revolution and were unimpressed. The antics of Francis Marion, aka the Swamp Fox (melodramatically portrayed by the legendary bigot Mel Gibson in the movie *The Patriot*), and the South Carolina militia were the exception, not the rule. General George Washington and his officers in the Continental Army considered them a necessary evil at best. One of those officers, Henry Lee III, referring to the battle at Guilford Court House, said, "American regular troops behaved there with the most gallant intrepidity. What did the militia do? The greatest numbers of them fled. …had the line been supported that day, Cornwallis, instead of surrendering at York, would have laid down his arms at Guilford."

Numerous letters and editorials exist related to the debate about standing armies, firearms, and militias; in none is a mention of private gun ownership by individuals.

Arms were considered helpful for two activities: hunting game and militia duties. Today the term "militia" refers to groups of gun nuts playing Rambo in the woods, but like many things, it meant something different in 1791.

At issue was a national army and the control of the militias. The Federalists, remembering the bumbling and cowardly performances of many militias during the revolution, wanted a standing army or a trained and regulated militia. The anti-Federalists wanted no part of anything resembling a standing army and the Second Amendment was an attempt to appease both sides. Neither side had any argument about private gun ownership outside a well-regulated militia. The other big fight was about what to do about the Pennsylvania Quakers, who had no militia and whose pacifist views would prevent participation in a national militia. An earlier proposed version of the Second Amendment included "including the body of the people capable of bearing arms" about the Quakers.

"Much has changed since 1791. The traditional militia fell into desuetude, and state-based militia organizations were eventually incorporated into the federal military structure. The nation's military establishment has become enormously more powerful than eighteenth-century armies. We still hear political rhetoric about federal tyranny, but most Americans do not fear the nation's armed forces and virtually no one thinks that an armed populace could defeat those forces in battle. Furthermore, eighteenth-century civilians routinely kept at home the very same weapons they would need if called to serve in the militia, while modern soldiers are equipped with weapons that differ significantly from those generally thought appropriate for civilian uses. Civilians no longer expect to use their household weapons for militia duty, although they still keep and bear arms to defend against common criminals (as well as for hunting and other forms of recreation)." [2]

So what did the founders think? Many things, and the only way we can know is through their correspondence. Let's start with some things the founders did not say but have been attributed to them by the NRA and other gun-rights organizations:

George Washington never said, "*Firearms stand next in importance to the Constitution itself. They are the American people's liberty teeth and keystone under independence ... from the hour the Pilgrims landed to the present day, events, occurrences and tendencies prove that to ensure peace security and happiness, the rifle and pistol are equally indispensable ... the very atmosphere of firearms anywhere restrains evil interference—they deserve a place of honor with all that's good.* The likely came from a 1926 article in a magazine called *Hunter-Trapper-Trader*." [3]

Thomas Jefferson never wrote, "The strongest reason for the people to retain the right to keep and bear arms is, as a last resort, to protect themselves against tyranny in government." This correction was from an article in the *Orlando Sentinel* in the late 1980s. [3]

Jefferson also never said, "The beauty of the Second Amendment is that it will not be needed until someone tries to take it." This quote is from a fictional Thomas Jefferson in the novel *On a Hill They Call Capital* (sic). [3]

John Adams would never have said, "Arms in the hands of the citizens may be used at individual discretion for the defense of the country, the overthrow of tyranny or private self defense." [3] I am not sure of this source, but it does not reflect Adams' distrust of unrest among ordinary people. I suspect someone from the NRA pulled it out of his ass.

Alexander Hamilton never said nor wrote, "The best we can help for concerning the people at large is that they be properly armed." This quote was from a pro-gun website that claimed it was from the 184th Federalist Paper. We know this is bullshit because there were only 85 Federalist Papers.

In his book *Guns, Crime & Freedom*, Wayne LaPierre argues that virtually all of the founders and anyone of importance at the time of the Second Amendment believed that everyone should be armed in the way the NRA prescribes. He also takes quotes out of context and misquotes several of the founders. [3] This is just LaPierre lying in print rather than his usual vocal medium. Bullshit is a trademark of the NRA and other gun nuts. I shouldn't lump the NRA in with gun nuts like that. The NRA is more. It is a shill for firearms manufacturers, and its members are only financial assets.

The founding fathers said and wrote many things, and frequently those "things" had to do with a federal army and militias. None of the recorded quotes mention private gun ownership outside a well-regulated militia.

SOURCES

Campbell, Jeffrey P. "Original Intent of the Second Amendment: What the Debates at the Constitutional Convention and the First Congress Say about the Right to Bear Arms." *Original Intent of the Second Amendment: What the Debates at the Constitutional Convention and the First Congress Say About the Right to Bear Arms*, Oklahoma State University, 1 May 2012, https://shareok.org/handle/11244/9064.

Lund, Nelson; and Adam Winkler. "The Second Amendment." *Interpretation: The Second Amendment | The National Constitution Center*, The National Constitution Center, 16 Aug. 2016, https://constitutioncenter.org/interactive-Constitution/interpretation/amendment-ii/interps/99.

Madison, James. "The Bill of Rights: A Transcription." *National Archives and Records Administration*, National Archives and Records Administration, 12 July 2022, https://www.archives.gov/founding-docs/bill-of-rights-transcript.

Reitz, Dan. "What Did the Founding Fathers Really Say about Guns?" *Medium*, Medium, 24 June 2022, https://danreitzdotcom.medium.com/what-did-the-founding-fathers-really-say-about-guns-9811cf7a6fdc.

Part IV: Religion

Chapter Ten: On QAnon

QAnon is a far-right-wing decentralized and loosely organized political movement founded on the belief that Donald Trump is secretly waging war against a satanic cabal of pedophiles. The members of this alleged conspiracy control the world, run a global child sex trafficking ring, and murder children to obtain a life-extending chemical from their blood. QAnon members believe that a purge is coming in which Trump will apprehend all members of the evil network and hold them at Guantanamo for trial and punishment. QAnon is an ever-evolving group covering a diverse set of other beliefs. Followers believe every president before Trump was a puppet of the conspiracy they call "The Deep State," and a group of generals recruited Trump to be the messiah who turns it all around.

Who is Q? According to the dogma, Q is one or more high-security-clearance intelligence operatives. This narrative is the least likely. Several people have claimed to be Q, and several potential candidates have denied they are. We can be sure of one fact. QAnon has its roots in the uncensored and loosely moderated world of 4chan and its successors. Manny Chavez, who goes by the gamer tag Defango, claims he invented Q as a live-action role-playing game. He claims the program grew out of an online puzzle called Cicada 3301. Not long after introducing the idea for Q, a rival, Thomas Schoenberger, stole the idea and made the game more radical. Schoenberger radicalized the project by adding iconography from the occult and Nazism.

The game evolved to include leaving clues, or Q-drops, to convince players they were figuring things out for themselves when the conclusion was predetermined and the clues were pre-seeded. In 2017, Lisa Clapier, a left-wing activist with the Twitter tag @snowwhite7Iam, encouraged Cicada players to "follow the white rabbit" to a new game and moved the action to mainstream social media.

Other possible sources for Q have also come from the "chans." Q was not the first "anon" poster. Other anons have been High-level-anon, FBI-anon, CIA-anon, White House-insider-anon, and others. 4chan and 8cham founder Fredrick Brennan became an open critic of 8chan and QAnon. As a software engineer and developer, he tracked the original QAnon drops to Jim and Ron Watkins. Jim Watkins provided hosting for 8chan and eventually wrested control and ownership from Brennan. Rod Watkins later admitted to being Q, an anticlimactic admission since Brennan had already made that claim. Jim Watkin's motive seems to have been to monetize 8chan, and QAnon seemed his best vehicle to accomplish that. Watkins created his new channel to challenge Breitbart, based on the Clinton body count memes, pedophilia, and the FBI impounding Democrats' laptops. Ironically, the track named *The Goldwater* failed because potential followers thought it was a Jewish site.

Disgraced former General Michael Flynn engineered the most blatant and successful attempt to profit from QAnon. Until taken down after January 6, many links on Q-related forums led to Flynn's legal defense site, where he sold Q merchandise. Given all the fabrications in which Flynn has engaged, it isn't easy to judge the sincerity of anything he does. Does he believe the wild conspiracies of QAnon, or is it just another vehicle for money and power? One can never know with Michael Flynn.

After a dispute with Watkin over the control of an 8chan sub-board known as CBTS_Stream (Calm Before the Storm), South African conspiracy theorist Paul Furber moved his renamed board, r/thegreatawakening, to Reddit and opened QAnon memes to the big leagues of social media.

The origin of Q is not essential other than to point out that Q was not the intelligence insider that Q adherents continue to believe he was. The source of the belief system QAnon allegedly created is of more interest. None of it is original.

The core belief in a group of child-exploiting elites is taken directly from the anti-Semitic canard known as "blood libel," the idea that Jews murdered Christian boys to use their blood in ceremonial practices. The Dominion voting machines manipulation conspiracy comes from the plot of *Man of the Year*, a 2006 film starring Robin Williams.

Adrenochrome is an inexpensive, easily synthesized drug, as easy as oxidizing the contents of an EpiPen. There is no need to harvest children's blood to obtain it, nor does it affect extending life more than adrenaline. Adrenochrome has been mentioned in sci-fi and other fictional accounts since the 1950s. It is said to have psychedelic effects in Aldous Huxley's *The Doors of Perception* (1954), Anthony Burgess's *A Clockwork Orange* (1962), and Hunter S. Thompson's *Fear and Loathing in Las Vegas* (1971). Adrenochrome was most recently featured in the eponymous film of 2017.

The Storm, or The Great Awakening, is also a very familiar concept. A day of judgment for evildoers is an overused plot element in books and movies that are too numerous to mention. And even the Bible says it in a few places, that The Storm never happened, unless you consider the botched insurrection, has not seemed to deter the belief among some QAnon members that it still will. Some members even believe that Trump is still secretly president and lining up all the suspects for the final judgment.

Then there are the lizard people. We can credit David Icke, former soccer player and BBC newsreader, for adding this conspiracy to the Q collection. Icke wrote his first book in a series of twenty books about the Archons, blood-drinking, shape-shifting reptilians from the Alpha Draconis star system, in 1999. The premise of Icke's book may sound eerily familiar to the television series *V*, which first aired in 1983. Icke has admitted to using the series as a source for his books. In a case of political fiction imitating science fiction imitating political fiction, the writers of the 2009 renewed *V* confessed to using Icke's books as a source for new scripts.

Human memory is notoriously unreliable. It has trouble discerning fact from fiction and past dreams from reality. It creates a familiarity with new assertions and a more powerful suspension of disbelief. It is much easier to believe something with which your memory makes familiarity, and I have already shown that most QAnon memes come from previous media sources.

Since QAnon is an informal and loosely organized group, there is no membership role, but we can make some general deductions about the membership demographics. Although the level of education plays a significant role, 57% have a high school education or less, and many members have advanced degrees. Instead of going away after the 2020 inauguration, QAnon membership increased to about 17% of the U.S. population and has remained steady since the end of 2021.

Around 70% of QAnon believers list their political affiliation as Republican (43%) or Independent (27%). The PPRI study did not attempt to break down associations by gender, but we know that women began joining in droves during the pandemic. Pastel QAnon was designed to appeal to women by focusing on the alleged abuse of children and generally softening the more militant messaging. Racism also plays a large part in QAnon's beliefs, and women are not necessarily the genteel pacifists we may imagine them to be. Women have played a prominent role in the white nationalist movement. This dominant image of the alt-right as a "manosphere," however accurate it may be, obscures the long history of white women's participation in white supremacy. As Nancy Love writes in *Shield Maidens, Fashy Femmes, and TradWives: Feminism, Patriarchy, and Right-Wing Populism,* "White women were active in the Ku Klux Klan, the American Nazi Party, and more recently, have joined neo-Nazi groups, such as the Aryan Nation, National Vanguard, White Aryan Resistance, and now the alt-right." Seyward Darby's book, *Sisters in Hate: American Women on the Front Lines of White Nationalism,* acknowledges that "White supremacist [movements] would collapse without women's labor" (Bloom and Moskalenko).

Media consumption is by far the most reliable predictor of QAnon association. Those who list right-wing news outlets such as Fox News, Newsmax, and One America News Outlet are five times more likely to be QAnon supporters than those who trust the mainstream media's new sources.

QAnon is predominantly an American phenomenon, but Q knockoffs have extended globally. So how did this concept of crazy beliefs and conspiracy ever reach the point that nearly one in five Americans are believers in either all or part of it? The participatory nature of QAnon is the answer. It may have originated as an interactive game and remained interactive as it evolved into a political movement. Participants are encouraged to decipher and explain Q-drops or create their own, which requires active participation. Involving people in these activities produces a sense of belonging and can quickly lead to acceptance.

Is QAnon dangerous or a relatively harmless distraction? Not all Q followers are prone to violence, but enough are that the answer must be a resounding yes. We have seen the ugly history of racism and found that any organization mainly founded on bigotry and hate is profoundly dangerous. The Ku Klux Klan has an over one-hundred-dred-year history of lynchings, murder, and violence.

Anti-Semitism has an extended history and is at the core of much of what QAnon believes. Much of the beliefs on which QAnon is based have come from *The Protocols of the Elders of Zion,* as has every anti-Semitic trope since the czarist secret police forged the document in 1902. Also known as *The Protocols,* the tract was allegedly written by Jewish elders in a cemetery in Prague. The document contains all the machinations erroneously attributed to Jewish people. There can be little doubt that the attacks against a synagogue in Pittsburgh, a kosher grocery in Jersey City, and the Hanukkah stabling in New York were inspired by these and other anti-Jewish works. While not all perpetrators are directly connected to QAnon, they all occurred after QAnon became mainstream. Of the 900 arrested for participation in the January 6 insurrection, at least 66 were identified as QAnon adherents by the Anti-Defamation League.

"A report mining criminal records of QAnon followers who were arrested for storming the U.S. Capitol on January 6 found an excessive number of them (68%) with documented psychiatric problems. These mental disorders ranged from depression and anxiety to paranoid schizophrenia, bipolar disorder, and PTSD. For comparison, only 21 percent of Americans had a diagnosed psychological disorder in 201948—a rate less than one-third of that among QAnon insurrectionists. The same report found that seven out of eight women who committed violence at the Capitol riot had experienced a psychological trauma that led to their radicalization" (sic) (Bloom and Moskalenko, p. 137).

All of this confirms my bias. I have always felt that a significant portion of QAnon supporters are batshit crazy and, therefore, volatile and unpredictable. Unpredictable is, by its very nature, dangerous as is volatile, which the definition implies. Knowing acceptable behavior and expecting it from others is the cornerstone of any society.

So, what do we do about this? The crazies mentioned above will require the help of trained professionals, and there is nothing the layman can do. The only antidote to misinformation is information. Factual information is where people like us can be helpful. When we see misinformation posted on social media, we can respond with the correct information and add a link to our source. Facts will not cause the hardcore cultists, and QAnon has become like a religious cult, to see the light immediately, but those who have not entirely gone down the rabbit hole will slowly respond. Returning as many believers as possible to reality is both noble and necessary. Do not insult or berate; this will yield negative returns. Post as if you were talking to a friend or, as Joe Friday used to say, "Just the facts, ma'am."

SOURCES

Bloom, Mia; and Sophia Moskalenko. *Pastels and Pedophiles: Inside the Mind of QAnon.* Redwood Press, an Imprint of Stanford University Press, 2021.

Gilbert, David. "QAnon Isn't Dead. It's Growing." *VICE*, 24 Feb. 2022, https://www.vice.com/en/article/93bg5a/qanon-conspiracy-theory-prri-poll.

Huff, Ian. "Four Myths about QAnon and the Movement's Impact on American Politics in 2022." *PRRI*, Public Religion Research Institute, 16 Mar. 2022, https://www.prri.org/spotlight/four-myths-about-qanon-and-the-movements-impact-on-american-politics-in-2022/.

Klepper, David; and Ali Swenson. "Trump Begins Openly Embracing and Amplifying False Fringe QAnon Conspiracy Theory." *PBS*, Public Broadcasting Service, 16 Sept. 2022, https://www.pbs.org/newshour/politics/trump-begins-openly-embracing-and-amplifying-false-fringe-qanon-conspiracy-theory.

Love, Nancy S. "Shield Maidens, Fashy Femmes, and Tradwives: Feminism, Patriarchy, and Right-Wing Populism." *Frontiers*, Frontiers, 1 Jan. 1AD, https://www.frontiersin.org/articles/10.3389/fsoc.2020.619572/full.

Staff, PRRI. "The Persistence of QAnon in the Post-Trump Era: An Analysis of Who Believes the Conspiracies." *PRRI*, Public Religion Research Institute, 2 Mar. 2022, https://www.prri.org/research/the-persistence-of-qanon-in-the-post-trump-era-an-analysis-of-who-believes-the-conspiracies/.

Next: On the Christian Right

Chapter Eleven: On the Christian Right

The destruction of the great Library of Alexandria has been blamed on many. It seems nobody wanted to come forward and take credit for the act. The first person blamed was Julius Caesar for the unintentional result of the firing of the Egyptian fleet. Others blamed the Christians for a desire to destroy all knowledge they deemed to be from pagan sources. The Christians attempted to destroy all records of Greek culture. Another charge is that it was done by Muslims when they moved into Egypt. The latter explanation can be dismissed as not meeting the known timeline, and the Muslims came too late.

The second explanation is least as credible as the first, mainly because it fits the modus operandi of the Christians of the day and the Christian fundamentalists today. A religion founded on someone called "The Lamb of God" has a very violent history. They also have a history of opposing knowledge not obtained from the Bible. Although men wrote the books and decided which works to include, the fundamentalists view it as the word of God. If you read the Bible, you will discover that God was confused or that different people wrote different parts without coherent guidance.

The United States, despite being built on the principle of religious disestablishmentarianism and free practice of any or no religion, our history has been marked with religious discrimination and persecution. Mormons, Catholics, and Jews each experienced periods of persecution, some of which continue to this day. And let us not forget the biblical support of slavery and that the theological descendants of these people are still active today in the Christian nationalist movement. One need look no further than congresswomen Lauren Boebert and Marjorie Taylor Greene to discover two public officials willing to support the fundamentalists.

Christianity has a long and continuous history of opposing the sciences. Other religions have experienced periods of suppression of science, but none can beat their track record. While the Islamic world gave us algebra, numerals, water pumps, kerosene lamps, and countless other early inventions, the Christian part of Europe was in the dark ages. They gave us elaborate cathedrals, fiefdoms, illiteracy, and other things of which the records are either sparse or nonexistent. The Church controlled all knowledge. The populace was largely illiterate and did not understand Latin. The clergy was their only source of information. Priests might later pass on the text of the service, and monks translated historical writings. No original manuscripts of Tacitus and Josephus exist, and it is unlikely they wrote some of what was attributed to them. Yes, I am saying monks might have lied.

I don't write this to favor any religion over another but to provide a background on the intolerance and ignorance of the church throughout its history. Yes, persecution of Christians persisted for the first three centuries of the faith's existence, but they wasted no time getting their revenge after that. Wars were waged to oust Saracens from lands they had inhabited for centuries. Unbelievers were tortured and put to death. The religion of the lamb quickly turned from "turn the other cheek" to "let's kick some ass" and has remained so since. The reformation was an attempt to reform the Church but brought forth new corrupt policies. I have always maintained that arguments about the interpretation of scripture are intellectual masturbation at their finest.

Every religion has its charlatans. Christianity has the bonus of a Holy Spirit who possesses someone (like a demon?) and can bring forth unique talents such as faith healing and the handling of serpents—I fail to see the benefit here. Other talents include talking in languages that no one can understand—again, what's the use?—and other wonderous talents. One talent that the Spirit dispenses freely is the ability to become exceptionally wealthy and create mega-churches.

More than insulting practitioners, this essay is about the merging of Christianity and politics. The fundamentalist Christians of the past seven decades seem to have decided they should take an active role in elections to create a Christian theocracy. Their efforts include associations with unsavory individuals and a willingness to lie, promote outlandish conspiracies, and demonize opponents.

It started a little tame. Billy Graham was an evangelical preacher who gained a lot of wealth and renown. He was called the pastor of the presidents and was friends with Eisenhower, Johnson, and Nixon. Mostly he was apolitical and non-controversial. His son is a right-wing nut-job racist asshole. This trend was part of the evolution of evangelical Christianity from the 1940s and 1950s to the present day.

Religion was a political issue before the 1960s, but the Kennedy/Nixon race of 1960 brought it again to the forefront. The United States had elected Protestants to the office for decades, and Kennedy was Catholic. The Protestant right began allegations that it was the same as selecting the Pope and that Kennedy would consult with the Vatican on every decision. Their charges would prove ineffective, but this was just the warmup act.

In 1964, Barry Goldwater struck a devil's bargain with members of the John Birch Society, a right-wing conspiracy-based organization, and evangelical Christian leaders. It cost him the election but marked the beginning of the proper alignment of fundamentalist Christianity with the Republican party. Every future Republican presidential candidate would seek their support.

By the 1970s, the evangelical movement had started on its way as a protest of the socially liberal elements that favored efforts like gay rights and the Equal Rights Amendment. Leaders like Pat Robertson, a Pentecostal charlatan, multi-millionaire, fraudster, broadcaster, and Christian leader, had jumped full force into the political realm. Along with Ralph Reed, evil Ken doll, founder of the Christian Coalition and current chairman of the Georgia Republican party, he threw his following behind candidate Nixon. The ties between the racist, homophobic, meddling Christian right and the Republican party were firmly made.

In 1980, politics and religion formally mixed in the establishment of organizations like the Christian Roundtable and Moral Majority under the direction of prosperity theologist Jerry Falwell, conservative activist Paul Weyrich, and others. These groups helped propel Ronald Reagan to the presidency against the reborn—but apparently with a birth defect—Christian Jimmy Carter. The political platforms of these newly created groups included anti-sexuality, support of apartheid, and smaller federal government—or, should I say, smaller secular government. Their goal was: a government that operates on evangelical fundamentalist ethics, a focus on the Bible as unerringly accurate, and a literal interpretation of both testaments.

The Republicans had to engage in a balancing act for the next several elections. They had decided they needed the Christian right but did not want to be associated with some of its craziest statements and positions. Do you remember Pat Robertson declaring that he saw a fetus in radar photos of Hurricane Katrina and claimed it was God's way of punishing the sinners and abortionists in New Orleans? Yes, that's right, God kills 1800 innocent people, primarily poor and black, because he is pissed about something he never even mentioned to any of his numerous stenographers.

This direct approach was considered "looney" correctly, and beyond the pale, the Christian nationalists adopted a more indirect approach. By 2016, they had disguised their aims as new issues such as "states' rights," "religious liberty," and the "right to dissent." The language may be different, but the goal remains the same, a national religion that permeates and controls the government at all levels. Democracy as we know it would cease to exist and be replaced with a theocracy like Iran's. There would be weak legislative and judicial branches with exclusively conservative Christian judges and a strong executive led by someone approved by a Christian leadership council. Christian nationalists are not fans of democracy. The results are too unpredictable and could result in non-Christian candidates taking office. The fundamentalists supported apartheid and other authoritarian political systems.

The nationalists have also changed tactics regarding religious instruction in schools. Their numerous efforts to include mandatory prayer—they claim it is voluntary, but peer pressure and pressure from those in a superior position don't work that way—have all been ruled unconstitutional due to the establishment clause. Now they have adopted new techniques to implement religious indoctrination in schools. There is an effort to make parochial schools taxpayer-funded. I don't know about you, but I would choose not to pay for education not based on facts.

The attacks on public schools include challenging textbooks and books in the school library. The Christian right has been trying to include creationism books as science texts for decades. Their failures to convince the courts that it is credible science and not a way to sneak unsubstantiated doctrine into curricula have forced them to try different methods, such as intelligent design. Intelligent design is creationism in disguise. The premise is that there are so specific and complex biological mechanisms that some trial-and-error processes like evolution couldn't have created them. They have even found trained biologists and scientists, both associated and unassociated with the subject, to write papers and publish books defending ID. There is a problem with nearly every one of these papers—I think all these would be more appropriate, but there may be one out there that I missed. They were not submitted for scientific peer review before publication, and those reviewed were dismissed as flawed. How could anyone believe the universe's creation took place in only six days, the world is only six thousand years old, and a forty-day rain made the Grand Canyon? It remains a mystery to me.

Despite all these setbacks, the Christian right has become more aggressive. They are seeking to ban books about the factual history of the United States, using the grad-uate-level program called Critical Race Theory. CRT will never be taught in K-12.

Should they get their way? Should any book that challenges their ever-changing moral code they want to be banned? Those children who don't conform to their ideal are considered morally corrupt and either not worth educating or someone in need of reprogramming. If it sounds fascist and authoritarian, it is. Theocracies are, by definition, authoritarian. It all depends on which zealot or group of zealots is in charge. If the Christian nationalists are in control, people in the LBGTQ+ community—I have never figured out why the Q was added—it seems redundant and insulting—will be persecuted. Therefore, I propose that right-wing Christian Nationalists be considered a hate group.

Okay, what started all of this? I have been wary of and have felt hatred toward the religious right for quite some time. That part is not new. Recently, a group called Lifewise Academy—yes, I know, "lifewise" is not a word, and so does autocorrect—came to our community. Three bubbleheads on our Board of Education approved, without discussion or public input, approved their proposal to provide off-campus religious instruction. The original proposal to offer the option to opt out of art, music, or PE class to attend met too much blowback as an insult to teachers—also never consulted. The proposal was then amended to include only library time. I prefer that schoolchildren spend time in an area where fiction and nonfiction are clearly marked, and I expressed that opinion in a letter to the editor. I will give you one guess as to who is going to run against one of the three BOE members during the next election.

So now you know why I chose to write this now when it has been bothering me for the last four decades. I believe the Christian right, Christian nationalists, or bigot Christians, whatever your preference, are an existential threat to our representative democracy. They want to be the sole deciders of national policy and control all the levers of power. Even Iranians are beginning to see what a terrible system theocracy must be. There needs to be a backlash to the Christian movement. Stop sheltering churches from taxation and exempting them from the laws any other business must follow. If you have seen the mega-churches and have a clue as to how much money churches have, you will know that they are very lucrative businesses.

The Christian nationalists have already shown a propensity for violence when clinics are bombed, schoolchildren are threatened, and they seek the support of armed insurrections. They should be listed as a domestic terrorist group and monitored accordingly. Finally, I don't know about you, but I am tired of all the churches asking me to help fund charter and parochial schools. I never signed up for this and believed it to violate the Constitution. If you want to instruct your child in anti-history and anti-science bullshit, you should pay for it and possibly face charges for child abuse.

I used an honors thesis by Lewis J. Nordyke of James Madison University as a source for some of the information used here.

Chapter Twelve: The Problems with the Old Testament

I find it puzzling today why many Christians are eager to embrace the Holy Bible's Old Testament. Jesus declared it the law or the old covenant, and his coming meant a new covenant. The old covenant no longer applied to his followers. The whole idea of the Son of God was that since the wages of sin were death, nobody succeeded at being without sin, and nobody asked to be alive—God chose to start that ball rolling. Jesus was here to atone for all sins; we could only attain salvation through him. One could use the old rules, i.e., the Ten Commandments, as nonbinding behavioral guidelines. Those passages related to the prophecy that a savior would come might be pertinent from a historical perspective. Still, the rest of the Old Testament was no more than a historical reference.

The Old Testament contains contradictions, inconsistencies, weirdness, and outright nonsense. Let us start with the favorite book of creationists, Genesis; as the name implies, it is about how everything began. A problem arises from the observation that there are two different accounts of the creation of the universe and all things in it and those two accounts are only one short chapter apart. In Genesis 1:1-31, God creates light and separates day from night on the first day but does not create the sun and stars until the fourth day, after making plants on the third day. Plants can survive one day without photosynthesis. In this version, man, woman, and animals are all created on the fifth day. On the sixth day, he tidied up man's and woman's homes and told them all plants were safe to eat.

In Genesis 2:4-25, God created plants before there was an earth or rain. Then he created only man, followed by the tree of knowledge. He told Adam never to eat from that tree. At this time, Adam does not know anything other than what he has been told, so wouldn't this be like pointing something out to a toddler and saying, "This thing of which you were previously unaware; never touch it?" Then God made all the animals and told Adam to name them all, which seems like it would have taken much more than a day. After that, he created Eve out of one of Adam's ribs, men and women have the same number of ribs, so the only theological explanation is that at least one rib is regenerative. Then Adam is told that when a man leaves his mother—a concept of which he would be unaware—he should cleave to his wife—again, Adam does not know male and female or wife; he only knows Eve as person #2.

A couple of final thoughts on the creation stories: Adam is said to have lived for 930 years, or about 16% of the Earth's entire existence, according to young creationists. And he did all of this without any form of entertainment. When God punishes, he means it. The other thought concerns incest. There were only two sons with which to start. How might either father children, or the better question be, with whom? Either daughters went unmentioned, in which case they mated with their sisters, or they had a super-cool dad who let them mate with their mother. Either way, we have a family tree that doesn't branch.

The next featured story is that of a worldwide flood. First, let us look at the reasoning for a global flood. God finds that men can be violent. God decides he does not like this, so he kills all the men and the innocent animals by drowning them. God must have been thinking about how tired he was after the first creation, so he decided to appoint someone to survive the deluge and replace everything. Then he says a man named Noah shall be his steward of the post-apocalyptic world. Noah is a holy man who occasionally walks around naked in front of his sons—but hey, what dad hasn't? God instructed Noah to build a wooden ship less than one-third the size of the *Titanic*. Into this ship, Noah was to bring one of every plant species and two of every animal species in the world. Remember that the creationists believe that humans and dinosaurs coexisted on the young Earth. Take a moment to ponder the logistics of this task.

The largest wooden boat recorded outside the Bible was just over 300 feet long; compare this to the ark's stated length of 450 feet. The 300-foot ships required iron strapping for support and required pumps because they leaked badly. Even if Noah had the shipbuilding skill to build this giant boat, it was both too big to be seaworthy and too small for its assigned task of carrying two of just the roughly 700 species of dinosaurs, let alone lions and tigers, and bears. Oh, my! Furthermore, what did everything and everyone eat? There were plants, herbivores, and carnivores on board; all were consumers, and there was no space for sufficient prey and plants to feed them all for half a year. God magically solves this last problem by telling Noah to gather and store enough grub for everyone—but again, with the storage problem, not a Glad bag to be found. Then there is the waste problem. I can only imagine how much shit just a pair of tyrannosaurus and a pair of triceratops could generate on such a trip.

The remainder of the Old Testament contains equally outrageous tales of long-lived men, cruelty, unbelievable events, misogyny, intolerance, God as an asshole, and garden-variety bullshit. If you had ever undertaken the Herculean task of reading the whole thing, just getting through the "begats" is mind-numbing, you would conclude that much of what you read makes no sense when taken together. And you would invariably ask, "Who could believe this?"

PART V: In Memoriam

Chapter Thirteen: My Brother Joe

There is no date when I first met Joseph Steven Workman since he was my eldest brother. Long before my earliest memories, he was another face among the new faces when I first became aware of his presence. As I got older, I regarded him as one of the most incredible guys I would ever meet. I was the usurper to my brother Bill, who probably viewed me as a roadblock between him and my mother. Joe served as my protector except at bedtime, when both brothers delighted in scaring me as I walked the hallway to my top bunk. This was a nightly ritual, and knowing it was coming only seemed to make it more terrifying.

Speaking of usurpers, our sister, Marsha, probably was the most aggrieved. She had a brief stint as an only child and was either very happy with the situation or desired a sister. Then came Joe, followed by two more boys. Now she had three brothers who spent their time picking on or ignoring her. Marsha was forced to seek solace outside by making friends outside the family. Of course, she had Mom, but three boys have a way of demanding a mother's attention whether they are seeking it or not.

Bill spent much of his time tormenting me, so I looked to Joe for support. I remember my grandparents telling me I didn't hate Bill. After all, he only teased me because he loved me. I can remember not believing either premise. I need to point out that our relationship changed as we grew older.

Joe became my hero and role model at preschool age. The fact that he attended school only enhanced his image as a knowledgeable sage. Joe and Bill would fight occasionally, and there was an excellent chance that I was the instigator. Ever the champion of the underdog, I would join in by attacking whoever appeared to be winning. This would puzzle Joe, who was usually defending me, and he would ask why. I didn't have an answer, but I suspect I didn't want to see either get hurt.

Joe was everything. He was good in school, athletic, and made friends easily with a diverse class of personalities. Joe's Little League days in Findlay were a time of fawning admiration for me. I attended every game, as did Mrs. Koehler—I am not sure if that is the correct spelling, but it was pronounced "Kaylor." Mrs. K. was at every game, and she acted as a scorekeeper. I remember she would call out, "Come on, Jody," and in most cases, Joe delivered.

Joe could do all the things I couldn't. He could hit, throw, and catch the ball. I wasn't even any good in a snowball fight. Even though he never owned a bat named "Wonder Boy," he was a natural. Joe seemed to have it made in Findlay, and then we moved.

Auburn, Indiana, was about a fifth of the size of Findlay and lacked any notable entertainment. In his usual manner, he made friends almost immediately. Despite his seemingly easy adaptation, I suspect this move started Joe down a self-destructive path. He seemed to lose some of his easygoing nature and become troubled. There was nothing blatantly apparent at first, but he was just not his old self. Don't get me wrong, he was still my hero; it would take much more than a few screwups to change that.

When we moved to Auburn so that Dad could take a new position at Cooper Tire and Rubber, Joe was twelve years old. He was thrown into a new middle school and my sister into a new high school, whereas I went to a four-room school within walking distance.

I got to see more of Joe at this time. I was small for my age, towheaded, and deemed cute by girls Joe's age. Joe also taught me the art of talking like Donald Duck, a practice our mother called tongue talking, which completed my grooming for the job of "babe magnet." I knew my role in this play and gratefully accepted the part for a chance to be associated with Joe.

When Joe reached high school, he was firmly established as the boyfriend of choice by the females of the class. I saw him less because he began hanging out with boys who could drive cars and obtain beer. Joe's struggle with alcohol began at or shortly after this point.

I remember the first time he got caught, which undoubtedly was not the first time he got drunk. Our house in Auburn had an apartment in the back, and I spent much time there. I was watching television back there on the night in question. There was a commotion in the front area of the house. I am unsure if someone came to inform me or if I was preparing to go to bed.

My future brother-in-law had brought Joe home, and too much noise was made trying to sneak him into his bedroom; some vomiting may also have been involved.

Our parents were either asleep or watching TV in their bedroom and were alerted by the ruckus. From my position at the bottom of the stairs, I was informed that I should put off bedtime for a while longer; I could hear our mother wailing and our father's low but heated voice. And thus began the cycle of alcohol and guilt that would mar the next three decades of my brother's life.

Joe's life became a series of terrible decisions. I never lost faith in my brother's coolness and sought to emulate him instead of shunning him. And thus began a series of bad choices in my life. I can't in good conscience attribute all these terrible decisions to my adulation of Joe. In a desperate effort to fit in, I also chose to seek the friendship and counsel of stupid people.

Joe made two terrible choices within the next few years. There is some debate about whether Joe was in on the scam; I am convinced he was, but by faking a pregnancy, he wound up marrying a local hillbilly, lacking brains but with ample tits. Joe followed up on this blunder by enlisting in the United States Marine Corps. He moved with his new bride to Camp LeJeune to complete the fuckup trifecta.

I can only guess what Joe's reasons were for these actions. Perhaps he just wanted to get away. He, no doubt, sensed that his parental approval rating was declining. Like the rest of us boys, he craved his father's approval for the remainder of his life. Our father was not mean or stern, but he could be slightly stingy with praise and positive reinforcement. The latter did not apply to me. I may have been the only child to whom Dad showed affection and pride. I may like to think I was special, but it is just as likely that he had matured somewhat by the time I was born. We sometimes forget that our parents were only in their twenties when we were born and were still learning. At least, that is the excuse I use when remembering the screwups raising my children.

I only became aware of some of the events of the following period in Joe's life decades after they occurred. I received some photos from Joe featuring his wife, Peggy, passed out with her head drooping toward the floor. I viewed that as a general sign of how things were going.

I know he was stationed in Okinawa and hiding from us that he was doing stints in Vietnam. Again, I received no confirmation of the latter until much later. Although I became distraught with him at the time and even sent an anti-war letter to him, I didn't stop loving and admiring him. I know his wife was cheating on him when he left the country. I also know he met a local girl named Miko in Okinawa. I didn't realize he was in Vietnam getting shot at while repairing radio towers when letters went unanswered for an abnormally long time. Perhaps in a desperate longing to live in the United States or out of genuine love for Joe, Miko did everything she could to grease the wheels stateside. She made a beautiful knit tapestry of a tiger for my mother, sent baked goods, and even wrote me a letter. It was not to be, but she was there for Joe when he needed someone, which is good enough for me.

I also remember his return to Ft. Wayne airport after his honorable discharge. While the family was on the tarmac, Baer Field didn't have gates in those days, Peggy and her mother arrived. We were treated to an act unworthy of any thespian award. When challenged about her infidelity, she immediately went into a swoon that fooled nobody except her mother. Joe went with her telling us he would handle the matter. A few weeks later, he was divorced.

Joe used his time after the divorce to decompress. Even though I had nothing to unwind from, I honored my lifelong tradition of doing what Joe did. Decompressing involved sleeping late, sitting around in long underwear during the day, and drinking or doing drugs at night. Joe and I were usually not together for these nighttime activities, but I remember one occasion when we were.

We were sitting along an infrequently traveled county road after taking some hallucinogens. In the Auburn area, hallucinogens were of unknown composition. One had to take the dealer's word as to its contents. It could be anything from oxidized Drano with a pinch of LSD or psilocybin to the real things. While sitting in the car, Joe insisted he saw something in the field in front of a row of trees. Whether it was because nobody else saw it or because we had been smoking weed and were suffering from a severe lack of ambition, nobody wanted to go check it out with him. Joe was damned determined to get to the bottom of this. I exited the car with him but had no intention of doing anything more. I finally asked if the person, animal, or object was moving. When he replied no, I explained that since we did not know if it was dangerous, it was better not to attract its attention. This worked, and we returned to the car, leaving the mystery unsolved forever.

Our father finally grew tired of us freeloading. I am not sure what he told Joe, but Joe moved in with someone whose name I no longer remember; I think he was Joe Lewis' younger brother. I got taken to a local watering hole in Hamilton, Indiana, and received the infamous "running away from home" speech. It seemed that he had decided that too many people depended on him, and the only solution was for him to leave and start a new life somewhere else. I should point out that my father tended to self-pity. It was a problem since childhood since I remember him telling me earlier that his best friend from childhood had said dad frequently felt sorry for himself.

Dad didn't move out, and Joe went on the road with fellow Vietnam Marine Corps veteran Pat Refner. The extent of their travels is not known to this day. I know

Joe had settled in Southern California for a while as I had bought an airline ticket to join him. After obtaining a position at the Fort Wayne Post Office, I reconsidered and had the price of my ticket refunded. Joe stayed with some Marine buddies in Texas, but I am unsure when or how long. I know Joe and Pat made their way to Eureka Springs, Arkansas, where they picked up some extra cash playing in the biweekly Passion Play. I know he brought a young woman home with him who was probably closer to my age than his. She stayed with us, in a separate bedroom, for a while, and I don't know whatever happened to her.

At about that time, Joe married Christine Brown, her name may have been Sprague then, and they lived together in Auburn. Chris had two children, Shannon and Brian, whom Joe adopted, although Brian later changed his name back to Sprague. Joe's daughter, Joie, was born a few years later.

I didn't interact much with Joe then, although I still lived at home and drove to Ft. Wayne daily. I gained employment in mid-December, so I worked 84 hours per week and still made the two-and-a-half-hour roundtrip commute daily. I didn't see much of Joe during this time. After Christmas, I remember bailing him out of jail two times. Once was for public intoxication, which I don't consider an actual crime. On another occasion, Joe had mistaken someone else's house for his and broke the door. I settled by paying too much for a new screen door and the fine.

I am not proud to say that I held this over Joe's head for several years after. He adopted the attitude that we were even since I was still living at home, and he had to pay rent. He also pointed out that he had not asked for my help on either occasion. Joe was willing to remain in jail for the public intoxication charge, but I didn't think that approach would work out well for the count of breaking and entering I prevented.

The incident that probably met the most disapproval from our parents was when Joe hit an oil tanker truck on a snowy county road while using their car. Although he was uninjured, the tanker and vehicle damage was considerable. Indiana was not a no-fault state, and the company that owned the truck sought to assign blame to Joe and the vehicle. Since Joe was not the car's owner, the surrounding legal shitstorm centered on our father. Dad hired a lawyer and avoided losing his driver's license, but the whole incident turned about to be expensive and damaged Joe's case for paternal acceptance.

Nobody could ever accuse Joe of being an overachiever. He had attended college in Fullerton, California, where tuition was free, and may have taken some classes in Fort Wayne. Perhaps because of his early responsibilities or his change in point of view that must have taken place after his stint in the Marine Corps, he chose not to pursue any further academics. Our congressman had chosen him as an alternate for the Army and Air Force Academies. Still, he decided not to follow up on either once he found out how many alternates had been named. Instead, he took factory jobs, including a lengthy stint at a Nucor Corporation. Possibly because he felt shame for neglecting to follow up on any college opportunities, Joe would resent those in the family who graduated from any college. He knew his intelligence was not holding him back and did not like the idea of others thinking they were smarter than him.

Joe and Chris lived in Auburn and St. Joe before moving to Island Park at Hamilton Lake, where I lived with my parents. Joe, like his brothers, was inexplicably ever seeking the acceptance and approval of our father. Since Joe drank a lot during that time, I did as well, approbation was not forthcoming, and he moved on. Through the trials and tribulations, Joe and Chris seemed happy together, and it appeared Joe had finally achieved a stable relationship.

Two events changed the paths of Joe's family and mine. First, I started a family by marrying the former Cathy Osbun and moving to Bowling Green, Ohio, to follow my father, who had taken a job at the new Cooper Tire and Rubber facility there. This was not the last job I would get using someone else's influence. Next, our brother-in-law and sister moved to Spring, Texas, where he found a job as vice president of a startup thermoset plastics operation. Since the northern states were suffering a recession, shedding automotive-related jobs, and the Houston area was experiencing an oil boom, it became an attractive place to live and work.

Joe, Chris, Cathy, and I drove Joe's van on a fact-finding trip to Houston about a year after I started my Cooper laboratory job. As a result of the journey, I found a job, and Joe discovered that jobs were plentiful there and came to Texas about a year later. Since Chris had never agreed to join him, it marked the end of Joe's second marriage.

Somewhere along the way, Joe teamed up with Joe Lewis, a fellow veteran from Waterloo, Indiana. They seemed an unlikely pair with different dispositions. It seemed the only things they had in common were a desire to live in Texas and drinking. Joe's daughters, Shannon and Joie, came to live with them, and since neither of the Joes could be considered responsible adults, Shannon had to be. She was young when she took responsibility for her sister, but she was up for the challenge.

I remember when Cathy and I visited Joe and Joe Lewis when they lived in an apartment in Round Rock, Texas. The visit had to be unpleasant for Cathy since the entire time was spent drinking and participating in high-risk rituals. Each Joe would stand on a second-floor railing and dive into the small swimming pool below. A slip or a short dive meant paralysis at best and death at worst, depending on one's perspective.

Luckily, when it came to my turn to try sobriety prevailed, and Cathy convinced me that it was a stupid risk that proved nothing.

Shannon eventually returned to her mother in Indiana while Joie stayed behind. In Texas, adults could bring children to a bar, where Joie found Joe's third and final wife. Joie probably just craved the attention that Kathy "I have no idea what her name was then" was happy to provide. I would later discover that Kathy would always have an ulterior motive. Kathy was never what anyone would consider a handsome woman. I think Joe was looking for someone to love and accept him the way he was, and since she was also a raging alcoholic, it seemed he had. Thus began a pattern of Kathy treating Joe's children malevolently while Joe was on the road, only to start treating them benevolently the day before he returned.

Joie, Shannon, and Kathy's son, Ricky, have no recollection of Kathy ever drinking. Whether she hid it well or was never an alcoholic, preferring instead to use alcoholism as another manipulation tool, as Joe's daughters suspect, cannot be proven. It is possible that Kathy had Histrionic Personality Disorder. She could adopt any regional accent depending on to whom she was speaking. Whatever her many faults, she showed Joe love, which seemed to be the object of his lifelong search.

This pattern continued until both children returned home to Hamilton. I don't know whether Joe ever knew how deceitful and calculating Kathy was, but she genuinely seemed to love Joe. I believe that Joe was so determined not to have a third marriage end in divorce that he overlooked much duplicity. When my mother had a heart attack, Joe moved to Jacksonville, Florida, to be closer to my parents living in The Villages. He could also continue the unending quest to receive our father's approval. He may have achieved it as he and Dad became close enough that Dad shared his regrets.

Throughout all of this, I never lost my love for my brother, and we kept in contact by available means. Since we lived a thousand miles apart, this often involved using some internet chat program or telephone. My mother said that no matter what end of the conversation she was hearing, she knew who was on the other end because Joe and I made each other laugh. I once told Joe about how my daughter, Amanda, had chosen me as the person who inspired her the most during her induction into the National Honor Society and how it made me feel so proud. Joe said I was an inspiration to him and the whole family. I may have teared up at this point, and it remains one of the highlights of my life.

I don't know who made the first step, but both Joe and Kathy began attending Alcoholics Anonymous meetings and maintained years of sobriety. I believe Joe did it for Joie and Shannon. He dumped out a full beer and quit alcohol when Joie was completing first grade. Joe worked for the local Interstate Batteries distributor. When he told the manager that he had to leave because hauling batteries to dealers had become too much for him, the manager gave him a desk job rather than lose him. I have always maintained that if Joe had the financing, he could have run his own business.

Despite his sobriety, much of the damage had already been done; he had Hepatitis C and liver cirrhosis. The only treatment then was similar to chemotherapy, making Joe more nauseous. With an untreated hernia, Joe's health outlook was not good.

Joie was set to graduate from Tri-State University with a bachelor's degree in Criminal Justice and Psychology, and everyone was in Hamilton to attend the ceremony. Despite the admonishments to hold applause until all graduates received their diplomas, we created an uproar when Joie's name was called. Despite any misgivings he may have had about college, Joe could not have been prouder. When we returned to Chris', Joe's ex-wife, not my son, who was aged in the single digits, house, Joe was very ill. His hernia had become infected, and he could not eat and was running a high fever. Out of concern, Shannon drove him to Parkview Hospital in Fort Wayne. The surgeons there offered to repair the hernia and cure the infection, but they were vetoed by Kathy, who was still in Jacksonville. I am convinced that this decision led to his death only months later. Despite his daughter's urging, Joe followed his wife's counsel. The physicians at Parkview treated his infection, and he was subsequently put on a plane back to Jacksonville.

Joe recovered enough to attend Joie's wedding about three months later. He was not well, and it was apparent. Our mother remarked on how ill he appeared. It had to be a desire to fulfill the role of father of the bride and to please his daughter that kept him going enough to walk her down the aisle and dance with her. This would be the last time I saw my brother alive.

It does not seem to me that it was long after his return that he required hospitalization again. While in one of the older hospitals in Jacksonville, Joe's organs began to fail. Bill and I took a flight to Jacksonville and rented a car to get to the hospital in time to visit. When we arrived at the hospital, we found his room empty and were told he had passed. This was not unexpected since he was not conscious when we last spoke to him on the phone. Still, a combination of shock and grief caused me to forget to ask if anyone had caught his pass.

Joe died on January 1, 2001. Kathy and our father were present. Joe's last words were "I'm dying, Dad," which haunted Dad for the rest of his life. No parent expects or wants to outlive their child. New Year's Day has never been a celebration for me since. I believe Bill and I found Joe's house mainly by accident. We had an address and no knowledge of the layout of Jacksonville. When we arrived, our parents, Joe's daughters, and my sister's family were already there. Kathy's idiot son, Rick, greeted me and began religious counseling I neither asked for nor wanted, complete with a defense of one of the Genesis creation myths. I spent the rest of the night outside in January, cold, drinking beer and smoking cigarettes. I had no desire to be part of the clown show I was sure was happening inside. I can remember being pissed off more than sad.

The funeral was well done, with a beautiful rendition of "Wind Beneath My Wings" accompanied by a slide show of moments in Joe's life, including a photo of him ready to bat in his Little League uniform. I was moved and declined to tell my story of being used as girl bait and loving every minute because it meant I could spend time with my hero.

Joe had sponsored many men in A.A., been sober for eighteen years, and was active in his church. Nothing about him was a disappointment, only potential unfulfilled. He loved and was loved deeply.

I will always think of Joe, especially as the end-of-year holidays approach. Although the concept of eternal life makes no sense to me, I am glad that Joe had faith to comfort him in his last days. I wish heaven were true; although eternity seems as extreme a punishment as it does a reward, too many good people die too young, and they deserve something better.

Chapter Fourteen: My Buddy and His Uncle Booj

I first met Todd in the summer of 1969 when his mother, and my sister, Marsha, brought him home from the hospital. I was an immensely proud uncle. Being the youngest Workman child, Todd was my first experience of being older than someone I cared about. We were living on Jackson Street in Auburn, Indiana. I know it was summer because I remember being shirtless when I first held him. He instinctively latched onto a nipple and began drawing off a dry well. When one is fifteen (about a month from his sixteenth birthday), his masculinity must never be left in doubt for a moment. I immediately went into defensive mode and began posturing great offense. I think I threatened to throw him to the floor if he tried again. Of course, I would never do that, but one could never leave any doubt about his total heterosexuality in rural Indiana in 1969. This was all for show, as he could not understand what I was saying and did something he did whenever a source was available.

Todd was only with us till the end of the year. Being a married man with a child pending did not prevent Todd's father, Don, from being drafted. He was stationed in the army at Fort Knox when Todd was born and came to take his family back to Kentucky in December of 1969. When I saw Todd again, our family had moved to Island Park on Hamilton Lake. In August 1970, Marsha and Todd came to stay with us on the lake. Don had a short leave while he prepared for assignment in Germany, the Vietnam War was still going strong, so it was the lesser of several evils. At fourteen months, Todd had officially entered the toddler stage, and I will forever associate the word with him, not just because of the similar sound but because of who Todd was. He looked so comfortable in his onesie pajamas that I envy them to this day, and he was the sweetest little guy I had ever met. Todd also had started asking for his Uncle

Booj, which further endeared him to me. Marsha and Todd left for Germany on Thanksgiving Day 1970 (a sad Thanksgiving for me), where I am sure that he became a star attraction among the army people stationed there. He returned a few weeks in March 1971. By then, he was a talking machine, albeit with the southern accent that seems to afflict all toddlers. He had the easygoing disposition he maintained for the rest of his life.

In April, Don's stint with the army was over. He returned to his job with Delco in Anderson, Indiana. Although I visited a few times, most of my information from the time was secondhand. Two significant events happened during the family's time in Anderson. First, instead of waiting patiently in his car seat, he drove the family car from the garage—taking a washing machine along for a few feet—through a fence and stopped just short of the neighbor's front window, hindered only by bushes and ice. Instead of being frightened, he seemed quite proud of himself. When Don reached the car and opened the door, Todd told him, "I drove the car, Daddy!" Second, his little sister, Tanya, was born.

The family left Anderson when Tanya was still an infant (about six weeks old) and moved to Chesterton, Indiana, where Don had a new job at one of the steel mills in Gary. It was a scary area for Marsha, so she drove home to Hamilton Lake frequently. I got to see Todd more, and he was getting to the point where I no longer needed a translator. Don was working from 3 P.M. to 3 A.M. They were so isolated in Chesterton that the neighbor's poodle was Todd's best friend.

Don and Marsha decided this was not the optimal place to raise children, so Don quit his job, and the family moved back to Hamilton. Don was promised a job at International Harvester in Fort Wayne, but when he went for the interview, the man who had made the promise no longer worked there, and there were no openings. So, he found himself unemployed with his family living in his in-laws' house. It was not ideal for him, but it was a great time for me. I saw Todd daily, and he was a joy to be around. Still proud of his driving prowess, he was a unique combination of cocky and kind. Even then, he was concerned with the wellbeing of others.

I enjoyed his company at this stage of his life. I am sure he could become angry, but I don't recall when he was. I heard secondhand about one occasion. As a toddler, Todd pronounced the digraph "th" as an f. The word "thing" would become "fing" and so forth. His father was frustrated with his efforts to try to get him to pronounce thunder correctly, shouting "Thunder, thunder, thunder with a t!" to which Todd, equally exasperated, replied, "Funder, funder, funder with a t!" He was his own man and could not be browbeaten into submission.

Although interested in activities I would have typically found boring, he had an amiable quality that made me feel better about life when I was around him. By this time in my life, I had already suffered what was politely called a nervous breakdown. I attended my graduation ceremony on leave from a hospital and still received an academic scholarship for any public college in Indiana. I would later blow the scholarship by quitting Indiana University in Bloomington after four weeks and Indiana University in Fort Wayne after one semester. Even though I did very well academically, I was in a dark place, and Todd brightened my life.

Of course, I had friends my age, and they would drive from Auburn sometimes so we could go out and do something pointless—which was an apt description of life in rural Northeast Indiana. I remember one occasion when Todd, Don, and I were playing something involving a ball in the common area in the center of Island Park. My friends arrived as we were playing and asked me to go with them. As I was walking to the car, I heard Todd urgently requesting, "Buce, come he-ah," I turned around and started back. My friends were getting irritated—Hamilton was not precisely on the way for anyone—and telling me to hurry up. Todd kept repeating his demand. I was torn. Don told me to go on, and I did, but with a reluctant sadness. I think I even gazed out the back window like some movie scene where you look back at someone you may never see again. He was incredibly loveable, and I didn't want to do anything to break that boy's heart.

Don found a job in Grabill, Indiana, and the Faylers moved into a house across the lake from us. After a brief stint in Fort Wayne, I moved back to my parents' place at the lake, where I remained until I was married. I had a lot of time with little to do. Todd was about four years old then and loved living at the lake. In the winter, he would get his dog, Spot—not a single spot on him—to pull him over the ice to Grandma's house. He thought this was the coolest thing in the world. Todd was still a little guy at this time. Tanya was about a year old, and her big brother was attentive and protective.

Many years before climate change was in full swing, we would put an ice shanty on the lake, either behind our house or in the neighboring bay. Lanterns in the hut provided enough heat that coats were frequently removed while fishing. I regret one occasion when a friend, Mike Carpenter, and I were ice fishing. Todd came out to the shanty to check on us and see if we needed anything in town, where he and grandma would soon be heading. We were low on beer—on the lake, there is no time when drinking is considered unacceptable while ice fishing—and we gave him some money and asked for a twelve-pack of beer, which Grandma would buy. The shack was on the ice in the bay, so it was not a short walk. Todd delivered the beer as promised and even included the change. I asked Mike how much money we should give Todd for his efforts. Mike immediately replied that kids that age thought a quarter was much money, which is what we should give him. I sheepishly gave Todd a quarter of the $2+ change he had given me and immediately felt terrible about it. Not only had I swindled a child, but I also did it to a child I loved. When we were done fishing and drinking— you can only pee in the holes so many times without wondering if that might be why the fish stopped biting—we locked up the hut and returned to the house. My mother immediately told us what cheap lowlifes we were. Upon remembering this event, I still feel bad about it. I only hope I did something later to make it up to him, or the alternative is to blame it all on Mike Carpenter, whom I will probably never see again since I have yet to attend a class reunion.

Keeping in my style of quitting anything that might lead to success—I was making more money than any of my friends and had built a nice nest egg—I quit my job at the post office to go on a quest to find America, or at least Indiana and west. It lasted about a month—I saw many things briefly. The interstate highway system was still incomplete, so I had to stop for a genuine cattle drive, and a cowboy waved at me. I had watched many westerns on our black-and-white TV when I was about Todd's age, so this was a special treat for me. Thank you, Wyoming, for being last on the infrastructure list! Since this was about the freest I had felt in my entire life, I could go on and on about the trip, but this story is not about just me.

Upon my return, I had a long stint of unemployment interrupted by brief periods of crappy jobs, and my old nemesis, depression, returned. My father tried to cheer me up by taking me to the local watering hole, where he told me he would leave and start over. He was tired of people depending on him and figured this was the only way it would stop. I love my father, but looking back, I can see that he tended to feel sorry for himself and adopt a "look at what you have done to me" attitude. A trait I have, no doubt, inherited. He also probably suffered from depression, but in those days, males could not admit to that. Only girls and women became depressed and could seek help—unless their fathers or husbands refused to pay for it. The talk changed little, except it may have made Dad feel better for a while.

I never failed to let an interviewer know that I didn't want the job. All the jobs, except one that I embarked upon throughout my career, were either the result of nepotism or by recommendation of Fred Pedersen, but that is another story.

In their efforts to stigmatize as many kids as possible, the Hamilton public schools had adopted a series of tests that a child must do to "graduate" kindergarten and proceed to the first grade—yes, you read that right, kindergarten! Todd could not pass the balance beam test—the Cold War was still going on at this time, so maybe they were screening for gymnasts to beat Olga Korbut. As a result of his poor balance—apparently, some five-year-old boys aren't a little clumsy—he was assigned to a remedial grade called "Reading Readiness" instead of the first grade. Of course, school-aged children not yet having learned empathy told him it was because he was slow. He was not, and it was the duty of all of us to remind him of that continually. I teased Todd from time to time—whether it was out of love or I was an innate asshole, I am not sure—but I never teased him about this. Todd did not do particularly well in school. At the time, I suspected he may have experienced some dyslexia. I was to change that amateur diagnosis years later, when Todd attended a Houston school training to work on aircraft engines. Anyone could tell he knew the material by talking to him, but he could not pass the written exams. There are psychological conditions known as test anxiety or examination stress. I believe this was a lifelong condition with Todd, or at least since he was labeled and degraded because of asinine first-grade requirements.

One of my periodic unemployment bonuses was the time I had for babysitting. When Don and Marsha wanted an adult escape, they called on me to look after the kids. If my somewhat foggy memory is correct, Todd would have been about five or six then, and Tanya three or four. Every time, they would tell me that their mom would make them milkshakes at night. I wasn't fooled for a minute, but I always complied. It may have been remorse for the beer delivery con mentioned earlier, or it may be that I knew keeping them happy would make the evening more effortless, or it could be that I liked milkshakes, too.

Todd's grandfather died, and Don inherited his business, Auburn Marine, and the end of my unemployment began. While working there, I hired my girlfriend/fiancée, Cathy, who became a babysitter for Todd and Tanya. The procedure was to drive Cathy to Hamilton. It was always a dual-babysitter situation. They would pull the same "Mom and Dad make us milkshakes" ploy. Cathy was highly doubtful the first time and would say that they never told her that. I had to step in and vouch for them. The kids and I had a "you lie, and I'll swear to it" relationship. I later explained the advantages of pretending ignorance to Cathy, and the ritual continued. We would call Cathy's mother a few times and tell her the road was too icy or some other excuse, and Cathy would spend the night. We would sleep on the bed in the basement near the heat pump. Sleep was the operative word here. Cathy was six years younger than me, and I was aware of the possible danger of criminal charges if the relationship went tits up. I have always wondered about the origin of this expression. It seems that "tits up" would be a desirable outcome unless we are referring to a cow.

Tanya was, and still is, an intelligent girl. She learned early on how to manipulate situations. From the time she knew how to play games, she was determined to win, and she was not above cheating. The usual scenario went like this: Todd and Tanya would play a board game. Tanya would cheat or win, honestly, but she nearly always won. Todd would accuse her of cheating, usually justifiably so. There would be an argument. Todd would smack Tanya, generally not hard. Tanya would scream as if great harm had befallen her. Todd was punished. I would explain that Todd was provoked on at least one occasion, probably many. Marsha and Don already knew Tanya would cheat at games, and the reaction was much greater than the action warranted, but the cycle continued. Things eventually changed, except for Tanya's "win at all costs" obsession, and they got along much better as they grew.

At about this same time, Todd wore his first pair of glasses. Nothing was unusual or esthetically unpleasing about his glasses, but I teased him about them anyway. I am still determining all the reasons for my banter. Still, I was trying to harden him to what I perceived as the mocking he would take from kids at school—I am now sure it was never as bad as I imagined—and teasing is also my unusual way of showing affection. Whatever the reason, he took it good-naturedly and even laughed.

When Todd was approaching his ninth birthday, situations changed rapidly. My father decided to take a job at the new Cooper Industrial Products plant in Bowling Green, OH. Cathy and I were married on June 3—Todd's contribution was to throw rice, overhand fastball style, with one or more grains striking me in the eye, so I spent the reception trying not to look like Popeye. We had moved to Bowling Green, where I worked in the lab due to nepotism. I didn't see much of Todd during the following year. There, my social anxiety got the best of me, and—mostly because I could not make friends—I became involved in the Church of Christ. Logic and reasoning eventually took over, and that phase of my life ended. After that, I would only attend church for weddings, funerals, or to appease a relative, which I eventually gave up.

In the summer of 1979, Don sold the Auburn Marine, and the family moved to Texas, where Don took a job as VP of a startup thermoset plastics fabricator. Realizing that there was no place for me to go at Cooper, Cathy and I followed in the fall. The job in Texas was the only time I found a job on my own. As a lab manager, I managed myself—I had no employees and had to assemble most of the lab equipment myself—at Bayou City Rubber, a part of Hydril. This privately owned company made equipment for the oil field. It was a Hydril blow-out preventer that failed to close during the BP Deepwater Horizon incident—I was long gone then and will accept no responsibility.

When we moved to Texas, we had no place to stay, so we stayed with Don and Marsha until we could find an apartment. After altogether wearing out our welcome, we found an apartment in the Greenspoint area, close to what was then called North Belt and is now part of the Sam Houston Tollway. We were about equidistant from the Fayler house and my work. Since we had no friends, we spent much time at the Faylers'. We later bought a mobile home and lived near Humble, Texas. My daughter was born at a hospital just inside the Houston city limits while I was doing my second job delivering the *Houston Post*.

Todd did better in a bigger school than at the small school in Hamilton. He could put the "Reading Readiness" fiasco behind him and start anew. Todd was always amiable and outgoing, so he never seemed to have trouble making friends. During the Texas years, I was able to watch him progress from elementary school to middle school.

Todd loved all beasts, great and small. At an age when other children wanted to be a fireman, an astronaut, or a cop, Todd wanted to be a veterinarian. He had a terrarium in his bedroom where he kept various creatures: lizards, toads, insects, etc., but not all simultaneously. It got to the point that his mother would not enter his bedroom for fear of what she might find there. Whether this was part of the point of this exercise or just an unintentional additional benefit may forever remain unknown. He preserved a bat that had flown into his car, probably due to defective sonar, in a formaldehyde-filled jar in his closet, where it remained undiscovered for several months. He even became angry with his mother for killing a scorpion she found in one of Tanya's shoes.

Todd's bedroom was also adorned with posters related to the band KISS. Of course, I had to tease him about this with all the knee-jerk Christian dogma—the band was a satanist front and assorted nonsense—as well as a few of my non-politically-correct creations. His response was always either to laugh or smile. Todd had a great smile. It was genuine and could disarm almost anyone.

By the time Todd entered high school, we had moved back and forth to Indiana three times. It took me many times to discover that my opinions about Auburn, Indiana, had not changed—it remained the asshole of the world—before moving to Mobile, Alabama. Our daughter attended kindergarten there, and we stayed in the Mobile area for a little less than a year before I accepted a job with Masco Corporation's R&D center in Taylor, Michigan. This job had some perquisites that previous jobs had not. I could travel at company expense and attend American Chemical Society-Rubber Division events. During my first spring there, the ACS had scheduled a meeting in North Houston, not far from where we used to live and close to the airport.

There was a meet-and-greet event after the day's agenda, where I could use the expense account for dining and drinks. I could fudge the report by using the names of others attending the event but not employed by Masco to treat the Fayler family. Marsha and Todd picked me up at the hotel. The area had changed since I had lived there; as it turned out, the "dine and drink" restaurants were further down North Belt. We drove to Fuddruckers for burgers and fries instead. We had a pleasant conversation. Todd had recently graduated from high school. I think this was when he told me he wanted to work on aircraft and would take courses on aviation mechanics at a Rice University extension. I assumed the realities of the cost of schooling coupled with the difficulty in making a living as a veterinarian had killed that dream, and he opted for something a little more pragmatic.

Todd loved being around family, and the takeaway from our dinner was that he told his mother he thought it was amazing that someone would forgo a company event to have burgers with his family. I treasure the moment because I would see less of Todd in the succeeding years.

The man who hired Don betrayed him, and the family moved to Bristol, Tennessee, where Don found a job in sales with another fiberglass fabricating company. Todd stayed in Houston for the next two years to finish his classes. Even though he had friends in the area, I imagine this was a lonely time for him with no family. Todd could not pass the final exam the first time, so he retook the course in the second year. He did not pass the second final exam. I am sure he knew the material as he told the instructor that he could pass the test if given orally. I am also confident that Todd was not "slow," as the first graders had told him. I believe that he was an intelligent guy who suffered from test anxiety or some mild learning disorder that made it harder for him to discern the meaning of written questions.

Todd joined his family in Bristol, much to his mother's relief. The Greenspoint area had degraded a lot since we lived there, and he was not in a safe neighborhood. Despite his disappointment, I think Todd was happier to be back around family. I visited once while he lived in the basement of his parents' townhouse. I could tell his cat, Miss Kitty—named after the character played by Amanda Blake in the television show *Gunsmoke*—had been well fed. Miss Kitty was big and fat in Garfield mode. If my memory is correct, he also had a critter or two in cages.

During this time, my parents, Todd's grandparents, had a home on Cordry Lake in Brown County, Indiana. Everyone loved to visit there, and I am unsure if this was why my father sold it and moved to Florida nearly as fast as he had bought the home. There was good fishing, and the swimming was okay in deeper water. I was determined to do some fishing on a rainy evening when the family was visiting. I asked if anyone would accompany me, and Todd was the only taker. We donned our ponchos and gear and trod out to the dock to try our luck. The rain was a heavy downpour, and the fish didn't want to bite on anything we were offering. It became an endurance contest that Todd won. I finally asked if he wanted to go in, and he agreed without argument. I am sure Todd wished to return to the warm, dry house as much as I did but did not say anything. I attribute this more to a desire to back me up than winning any real or imagined contest. He was just that kind of guy.

A few years later, the whole family met for Tanya's wedding. I met Todd's latest girlfriend for the rehearsal and dinner during the evening. She was a cute petite blonde named Terri. I remember thinking that Todd must be a stud, or at least he could get girls like I never could. It was not until after the dinner that I learned she was five years older than him and had a twelve-year-old boy and a little girl. I am sure Todd would have made a great father even with stepchildren and his young age, but the relationship was doomed to failure. While Terri was living with Todd, he kept a tarantula—they are not that dangerous, but the bite can hurt—and a pot-bellied pig that lived in the garage at night but was free to roam around the house during the day. Think of Todd as a "Tiger King" with a big heart, not a criminal, not in it for the money, and not gay.

Then Todd met Terri, and the creatures were gone in short order. The animals seemed to take it well, but the woman did not take it well at all. She spent the next couple of years trying to destroy Todd's reputation and credit. I view this as a lesson to young men everywhere: A woman can be a beauty and batshit crazy simultaneously.

Then Todd met Kristi, a ginger chick who reminded me of Sarah Ferguson, the Duchess of York. They married, and Todd jumped into the life of a married man. Don had told him that he was the end of the Fayler name, so Todd became a man with a mission. He adopted Wesley. Although I am not sure when the adoption became official, he started the process almost immediately. Then to ensure that the Fayler name continued for at least one more generation, Todd sired three sons and left no doubt about paternity. Even when very young, the three boys looked incredibly like him. There is another fact about Todd of which I am sure. He loved his family very much, and they became the center of his life.

I didn't see much of Todd in the intervening years. I was in Michigan, and he was in Bristol, Tennessee, then Virginia. Hindsight is 20-20 and also leads to much regret. Todd was almost fifteen years younger than me, and I assumed he would outlive me and that there would be plenty of time to reconnect. I had a way too brief visit with Todd before he was married. Cathy, Amanda, and I were coming back from my parents' house in Florida when we decided to take a side trip to Bristol. We did not intend to spend the night. I think I had to make that promise to gain a consensus on the side trip—but I don't think we made that apparent when we arrived. We met with Don and Marsha and, later, Todd. After visiting in Bristol for a while, we drove to Johnson City. We stopped at an Applebee's there, where Tanya worked. We looked at our watches as we talked, hoping to return to the road soon. As it turned out, we should have stayed. There was a big race in Lexington that day, and there was no room at any of the inns between the TN/KY border to well north of Cincinnati, so I had to drive straight through to Wyandotte, Michigan, arriving home at around 4 A.M.

The last time I saw Todd alive was at my brother's funeral. Bill and I arrived at the hospital shortly after Joe had died. My brother had married the homeliest woman in the world, who was also a slob and master manipulator. I stayed at my brother's house. While there, I spent most of my time on the back patio in the cold, where I drank beer, disrespected the widow, bitched about her eldest son, and eventually cried after I had had enough beer to remember I had lost my childhood hero. Todd and Kristie were much wiser and stayed in a nearby hotel.

Todd had come earlier and visited while Joe was still alive. When the end was near, I called the hospital to talk to him. I knew he was no longer conscious, but I thought I could at least say goodbye. Kathy, Joe's wife—I wondered if someone who had been sober as long as my brother could still be suffering from "beer goggles"—told me that he was becoming agitated, so she needed to end the call. I wondered if it occurred to her that he might be upset because he knew his life was ending.

I am unsure if this occurred before or while I was hiding on the patio, but Todd had discovered a bag of weed and a pipe in the garage. I have heard that, in some cases, marijuana is the only drug that can help with nausea and discomfort that come with liver problems and many other ailments. After the funeral, we met near their hotel, along with Kathy's youngest son, Jeff, to pay homage to Joe by smoking his weed. Kristie may have smoked, but I am sure she did not inhale. A sad day ended with laughter and a sense of closure. I was not angry with anyone, which is why I told Jeff some things I am sure he repeated to his mother. Of course, I did not know this was my last time with Todd, but I went away happy. Even though he was bigger than me, he was still my little buddy whom I had gotten to sleep with stuffed animals, balloons, and a few sips of my beer. At least I have comfort that I did not make him an alcoholic.

When I heard that Todd has MS, I was sad. It never occurred to me that MS could be fatal. I had never heard of anyone dying from MS. I thought it was a setback that could be cured with TLC, and he would still outlive me. A month later, I was shocked when I heard he had died. Something would be missing in my life. I was also angry. How could this have happened? It had to be due to gross medical incompetence. Someone should sue the bastards!

The funeral was the saddest event I had ever attended. When one of Todd's young sons asked why they were putting his daddy in the ground, it was more than I could bear. It was all so unfair.

My grief has since passed, although writing this has renewed some of those feelings. To this day, I wonder how much working around lead had to do with his untimely death. Unless you work for an organization where profit is not the sole motivation, like the CDC, any job requiring a hazmat suit can't be good for one's health. Today I have fond memories to temper the loss and regret. I have heard that only the good die young. I know that is true in this case, but I hope it isn't true in general. We need the good to stick around, and we could do with less evil. Also, since I am 68 and still going, I am unsure what the adage says about my character. There is one statement I can make with absolute certainty; in addition to being an all-around great guy, Todd Charles Fayler was the kindest person I have ever met in my 68-plus years.

Chapter Fifteen: Rex Deetz

Yesterday I learned that one of my oldest friends, Rex Deetz, had died. His death was not COVID related but resulted from a rare disease he had for several years. We first met when we were both eight years old; Rex was 31 days older than me. Our ages, along with our proximity—we lived three houses away from each other—and a shared love of the Detroit Tigers made friendship inevitable. We met in the late summer of 1961, and both attended Riley School, grades K-4 with one classroom each. We were part of the last third-grade class to learn at that school. I can't recall the names of all the students in that class, but Robin Opper could recite them decades later. Robin was another of my closest friends who died a few years ago. The ranks of survivors are getting low.

You could call Rex my BFF, but neither of us would have used that term. It reeks of femininity and would never be in accord with the macho images we were trying to project. You could call him my best friend, but we have collected many of those over the years.

This is one of the disadvantages of growing old. We spend too much of our time grieving for those we loved and lost and mourning for our lost youths when we took for granted that they would always be with us. It nullifies our memories as if our early life has lost its legitimacy. It is a sadness that matches the loss of my brother.

After I moved away from Auburn, Rex and I would always get in touch on our birthdays. I did not do that this year and can't say why. I thought there would be more "next years," or I would finally visit in person after so many years. I can add regret to my grief.

My visits to Auburn were rare and mostly to visit in-laws. After the death of my mother-in-law, the calls became less frequent, with my last being my father-in-law's funeral. Auburn is an excellent place to be from. I never liked it there and probably wouldn't have made it without Rex. Rex was a caring and reliable friend who did whatever he could for a needy friend. He was there for me through the highs and the lows. I miss him dearly, and my biggest regret is that I did not spend more time with him when I had the chance. Goodbye, Rex.

PART VI: Assholes of the Week

(These are for entertainment only and should never be confused with factual biographies.)

Chapter Sixteen: Jittery Jim Jordan: Asshole of the Week

James Littleman Jordan was born in 1964 to an iterant honey dipper and a 4H white ribbon sow. Jim attended the Graham Schools special education program in Saint Paris, a shithole town in West-Central Ohio. Due to the safety requirement that he must always wear wrestling headgear his head and an athletic supporter over his head, he was mercilessly teased by his schoolmates. Some taunts included "pipsqueak," "sack head," "pigmy," "shithead," and "shit for brains."

Jim showed an early fondness for close contact with scantily clad boys, so he became a wrestler while attending Graham High School. Since he was in the fart weight division, he won most of his matches by forfeit. Jim won state championships all seven years in high school. He graduated with outstanding effort honors and was accepted into the University of Wisconsin on a wrestling scholarship. He had porked up to the 134-lb. weight class and finally got to fulfill his fantasies about touching young men and being touched by young men in areas near the genitals. That's right; he was 134 lbs. or less when he won NCAA titles by wresting other tiny young men.

Although he will never admit it, it has long been rumored that Jim was and remained a closeted homosexual. This may explain his long record of homophobic remarks and opposition to any attempt to legitimize gay marriage or the LGBT community.

After graduating *cum ignominia* from the University of Wisconsin with a bachelor's degree in Economics, Jim transferred to The Ohio State University with the hope that he could maintain contact with muscular young men while pursuing graduate degrees. He worked as an assistant wrestling coach and attended classes toward a master's degree in Education. He kept wearing a jock on his face and headgear in private because he enjoyed the smell of scrotum sweat. Jim noticed everything as a coach except for the molesting of wrestlers by the team physician, even after some wrestlers told him about specific incidents. Perhaps his fear of being outed caused his memory loss, or maybe it was the strain of pursuing a Juris Doctorate with no intention of practicing law.

Jim did not need to pass the bar exam. The law was not the career for which he was looking. He wanted something easy, like looking the other way while student wrestlers under his care were molested. He wanted a job where moral courage was not a requirement. So, he chose to hold political office in gerrymandered Republican districts as a career.

Jim was elected as the Representative to the Ohio House in the safely gerrymandered 85th District in 1994. He served there without distinction for the next six years. In 2000, he won a seat in the U.S. House of Representatives that the same Republican had held for twenty-six years. Jim has never been in an election that wasn't a sure win for any Republican candidate. Ohio's 4th District contains a substantial population of moronic hicks, ensuring success for any right-wing candidate with a pulse. Said hicks are easy to spot in the towns and villages of the district by the cars with handwritten, misspelled, and idiotic memes prominently displayed.

Jim's anger at losing the opportunity to touch the genitals of young men revealed itself in his actions in Congress. He quickly aligned himself with other sexual predators, such as Mark Meadows and Mo Brooks, to form the Freedom Caucus. As a member of this caucus, Jim did his worst deeds, much to the delight of the morons back home.

He drove the Republican Speaker of the House, who called him "a legislative terrorist," to resign. He voted consistently against any bill that might help the middle class and poor in his district and the United States. He badgered witnesses testifying to the committees on which he served and generally acted like the asshole he is.

In 2015, Jim found his pacifiers. He began regularly performing fellatio and rim jobs on Presidential Candidate Donald Trump, a practice that continues today. His attachment to Trump led him to become his most prominent defender. Jim has outrageously denied ever hearing the pathological liar Trump tell a lie during an interview with Anderson Cooper. He has badgered witnesses testifying against Trump with loaded questions, interrupted answers, and what he perceives as intimidation. Due to his diminutive stature, it would be comical if it was not dangerous due to abuse of congressional power.

Jim employs the same modus operandi for every confrontational situation. He appears without a suit jacket, possibly believing his once-developed upper-arm muscles will be intimidating. He speaks loudly while feigning righteous indignation about whatever issue is under discussion. He takes a prosecutorial tone that he learned from watching episodes of *Law and Order*; keep in mind that he has no experience as a lawyer of any kind. He asks leading questions and interrupts answers with follow-ups or critical comments. He goes beyond the allotted time, attempting to prove a pointless point.

Since he is against anything newer than the Alien and Sedition Act, it is easier to list those things to which he is opposed. Jim views any attempt to ensure medical care to Americans that cannot afford it as a slippery slope to communism. To be more precise, he considers any program designed to help the average American socialist.

Jim opposes the implantation of the Affordable Care and Patient Act or any measure to modify or update it. He is against enforcing limits on carbon dioxide, tax incentives for renewable energy, and curtailing oil and gas exploration subsidies. Jim has sponsored a bill to amend the Constitution to ban same-sex marriages, but none of his bills seem to go anywhere. He supported a bill to allow voters to decide if they want their taxes raised.

Among his acts of assholery is the accusation that the ten-year-old rape victim was compelled to go to Indiana to get an abortion was a lie perpetrated by Planned Parenthood. When confronted with the rapist's confession, he retracted his accusation without apology. Jim is against abortion and funding Planned Parenthood. Perhaps he suspects he was tiny and ugly enough at birth that his sow mother wanted a retro abortion.

Jim is heavily involved in attempts to overturn the last presidential election results. He has adopted and supported outlandish conspiracy theories worthy of the craziest QAnon supporter. He uses committee assignments as a bully—although using "bully" and "Jim Jordan" in the same sentence seems ridiculous—pulpit for the absurd. There appears to be nothing he won't do to serve Trump. Could it be love? There are even allegations that he worked in support of the January 6 attack on the Capitol.

Jim has reveled in the narrow victory that propels him to the leadership of the Judiciary Committee. He announced plans to begin revenge investigations in retaliation to legitimate investigations of his dear, darling leader. Why he expects anyone to respond to congressional subpoenas that he has himself ignored is beyond comprehension. I hope he proceeds down this path like I hope Mike Lindell is selected as RNC leader.

Jim Jordan is a piece-of-shit professional politician who is deserving of an Asshole of the Decade award.

SOURCES

Johanek, Marilou. Ohio Capital Journal, May 3. "Jim Jordan Was Deeply Involved in the Attempted Coup to Overturn the 2020 Election." *Ohio Capital Journal*, The Ohio Capital Journal, 3 May 2022, https://ohiocapitaljournal.com/2022/05/03/jim-jordan-was-deeply-involved-in-the-attempted-coup-to-overturn-the-2020-election/.

Kolesnik, Kris, opinion contributor. "Why the GOP Oversight Agenda in the New Congress Likely Will Backfire." *The Hill*, The Hill, 29 Nov. 2022, https://thehill.com/opinion/white-house/3754608-why-the-gop-oversight-agenda-in-the-new-congress-likely-will-backfire/.

Wikipedia, Contributor. "Jim Jordan (American Politician)." *Wikipedia*, Wikimedia Foundation, 6 Dec. 2022, https://en.wikipedia.org/wiki/Jim_Jordan_(American_politician).</.i>

Chapter Seventeen: Donald Trump Jr.: Asshole of the Week

Announcing the MBW Asshole of the Week award winner: In recognition of excellence in assholiness and total indifference to the values of others, the winner is the sleazeball son of a scumbag former president: Donald John Trump Junior.

Junior was born on New Year's Eve, 1977, to Donald J. Trump and Ivana Zelníčková Trump—although Don Jr. remains on a continuing quest to discover the identity of his mother. He was the first child known to have been born with no will of his own. The latter condition was uncovered by his wet nurse, who noticed he would not cry, no matter how hungry he got, without permission from his father.

Although admitted to the finest private schools, Junior spent much of his education seated in the corner of the classroom and wearing a conical hat. Despite proclamations from his teachers such as "not the sharpest knife in the drawer" and "the gates are down, the lights are flashing, but there is no train coming," Don Jr. was admitted to the University of Pennsylvania, proving that money is still more important than test scores.

He received his B.S. in Economics and an A.D. in General Scummery and Politics. After college Junior went on to a distinguished career as the chief lackey for his father. Don Sr. began referring to him as his favorite pawn and his "go-to guy for taking the fall." Senior gave him meaningless roles and titles to distract him from his real job as the designated convict.

DJ became so proud of his pseudo-responsibilities that he forgot he was stupid and began to take himself seriously. He engaged in public speaking, which initially consisted of various grunting sounds. He became a much better speaker when his speeches were either dictated by his father or written by his sister.

The results were rambling tirades mixed with insults aimed at, in his words, "those meanies who want me to wear the pointy hat again."

In his personal life, Donny was able to attract girls with his witty pick-up line, "My daddy is really rich." A similar approach had worked on all his potential mothers—he hasn't ruled out Melania yet.

Mindful that he had done nothing on his own to become an asshole of his father's stature. Junior began some "covert"—easily discovered; remember, this is Junior—operations of his own. During the run-up to the 2016 election, he arranged a meeting with a not-so-secret agent to get dirt on Hillary. He soon discovered his contact was like all the other women he had met and only wanted money. There was no dirt, prompting others at the meeting to mutter something about a dunce and sitting in a corner.

During the midterm elections of 2018, Don Jr. campaigned for every douchebag running for office, including notorious pedophile Matt "I like 'em young" Gaetz. Days before the election in 2020, Junior sent messages to White House Chief of Staff Mark Meadows, discussing his plan to ensure his father remained president regardless of the outcome of the vote.

It was his work supporting the "Big Lie," having his crappy book buoyed by the sales of $300,000 of Republican donor money and copying the "bearded greaseball" look from Ted Cruz that finally qualified him for Asshole of the Week status.

So, congratulations go to Week 5's despicable winner Don "Help Me, Daddy" Trump Jr.

Chapter Eighteen: Extraordinary Elon Musk: Asshole of the Week

Although he has a weaselly appearance, both Elon's parents are homo sapiens. Elon was born in apartheid South Africa. His father was a white South African electromechanical engineer and property developer who owned a half-interest in an emerald mine. His mother was a Canadian-born model and dietician. Both are alive and retired. Elon Musk's story is not one of the rags to riches. His family was wealthy and gave him all the advantages.

Elon was a weird kid. At an early point in his childhood, South African doctors removed his adenoid—it is just one gland—because it was suspected that he was deaf. His mother later explained that he was thinking "in another world"—a practice that apparently continues to this day. There is no doubt that he was an intelligent child. His parents bought him a Commodore VIC-20 at the age of ten. He taught himself how to program by reading a manual and developed a BASIC-based video game, which he sold for $500 at the age of twelve. Elon was socially awkward and was bullied at school. In one case, he was hospitalized after being thrown down a flight of stairs by a group of boys at a preparatory school.

Elon wanted to go to the United States and knew it would be easier to do it via Canada. He applied for a Canadian passport using his mother's background. After graduating from an all-boys high school, he became eligible for military service in South Africa, so he attended the University of Pretoria to gain an exemption while waiting for the completion of the paperwork for his passport.

Elon lived with a cousin in Saskatchewan for the first year after arriving in Canada. As hard as it might be to imagine him doing anything like manual labor, it is said that he did odd jobs in and around a farm and a lumber mill while staying with his cousin.

He attended Queens University in Ontario for two years before transferring to the University of Pennsylvania. He graduated with bachelor's degrees in Physics and Economics from the University of Pennsylvania, the latter from the famous Warton School. He served two internships in Silicon Valley startups in 1994 and 1995 and was accepted into Stanford's Ph.D. program in Materials Science. Elon applied for a position at Netscape but received no replies to his inquiries. After two days, he dropped out of Stanford and decided to create a startup. He founded Zip2 with his younger brother, Kimbal, and Greg Kouri using Daddy's money. When Zip2 was sold to Compaq, Elon received $22 million.

In 1999, Elon founded X.com, an online financial services and email payment company. X.com was later merged with Confinity, an online bank founded by Peter Thiel and Max Levchin, which included PayPal. Musk became CEO of the merged company. His preference for Microsoft software over Unix caused a rift, and Thiel resigned. The resulting technological problems and lack of a coherent business model caused the board to oust Musk and replace him with Thiel, who renamed the entire company PayPal. When eBay acquired PayPal in 2002, Elon, as the majority shareholder, received $175.8 million. The whole adventure was a contest between Musk and Thiel as to who could be the bigger asshole.

After failing to acquire ICBMs from Russia to transport his Mars greenhouses, Elon decided to build his rockets and formed SpaceX. He became its CEO and Chief Engineer. After three failed launch attempts that nearly bankrupted the company, SpaceX was able to put a Falcon 1 into orbit in 2008 and was awarded a $1.6-billion supply contract with NASA. SpaceX has had many successes since then and launched over sixty satellites to form the Starlink satellite internet access program. The program has received criticism from the International Astronomical Union for blocking views and creating more opportunities for collisions. During the Russian invasion of Ukraine, Musk made Starlink available to the Ukrainians while refusing to stop Russian media broadcasts. He declared himself a "free speech absolutist."

Contrary to public perception, Elon was not a founder of Tesla Motors. It was yet another company in which he used his vast reserves of money to become the largest shareholder and weasel his way into the chairman of the board position.

Although he claims to be nonpartisan, most of his recent decisions, actions, and statements have favored the far-right branch of politics. His bid to control a significant social media outlet should concern us all. This "free speech absolutist" has announced his intentions to allow right-wing propaganda back on Twitter when he buys control. We will no longer be dealing with a corporation with a board of directors but private ownership by a single individual. This will be the worst thing to happen to public media since Rupert Murdoch and William Randolph Hearst.

Elon Musk is not a self-made billionaire. There is no such thing. He has used the advantages of birth into a wealthy family and the resulting monetary advantages to build and control powerful entities to do his bidding. He is the antithesis of altruism and serves only himself. He is a Grade-A asshole.

The background information is courtesy of Wikipedia.

Chapter Nineteen: Marjorie Taylor Greene: Asshole of the Week

We are announcing the MBW Asshole of the Week award winner: In recognition of excellence in assholiness and total indifference to the values of others, the winner is the inglorious MJT herself, Congresswoman from Georgia's 14th District and all-around crazy bitch: Marjorie Taylor Greene—Mrs. Greene has not done anything special this week or last but was a candidate any week and a nominee for the lifetime mendacity award.

Marge was born in Middleville, Georgia, on May 27, 1974, to kudzu farmer Robert Taylor and a bitch wolf—seldom do I find a case of "But who is the mother?" Still, as near as I can see, there is no mention of her anywhere, and Greene has only publicly referred to her in the collective parents. She graduated from the University of Georgia with Insanissimae Canis Femina honors. To earn money in college, she became a part-time prostitute. Her career in this field ended shortly after her passion for packing heat and shooting clients in the genitals was discovered. This passion, combined with the fact that a BBA degree is essentially worthless, led her to marry local idiot Perry Greene. In 2002 Margie's daddy sold his general contracting company to the Greenes. Midge was named vice president and CFO of the company, but an *Atlanta Journal-Constitution* investigation found she did almost nothing and had no significant presence at the company. She stepped down as CFO in 2011, a move that went unnoticed by everyone, including the president, to begin CrossFit training. Marge cofounded a gym with someone she met at a gym. She left the business in 2017, admitting that her BBA taught her little about running a business.

Armed with useless knowledge and a preference for doing as little as possible, she became politically engaged during the 2016 presidential primaries. She wrote articles for a conspiracy news website and a pro-police fake news website. She had found her calling: spouting outrageous lies, whether spoken or on paper. Her passion for gun violence, a propensity to lie that almost matched Herr Trump, and total indifference to her constituents made her the perfect candidate for the inbred rednecks in Georgia's goiter-filled 14th Congressional District. She topped the list of eight lesser evils and got 74% of the vote running unopposed in the general election—could we look at this as 26% of the voters finding no representation preferable to her? Marge became a member of the U.S. Congress after taking the oath to protect the Constitution with her fingers crossed on Jan. 3, 2021. What she did between then and the insurrection three days later remains undetermined.

As a congresswoman—gender not confirmed—she has done her absolute best to spread lies and misinformation at every opportunity. She has violated numerous congressional protocols and shown no inclination to support the Constitution or democracy. Marge was stripped of committee assignments. A resolution was proposed to expel her, though this is unlikely to get the two-thirds majority required.

So congratulations to this week's winner of the coveted MBW Asshole of the Week Award, Senior Space Cadet, and honorary Chief Crazy Bitch: Marjorie Taylor Greene.

Chapter Twenty: Ted Cruz: Asshole of the Week

I am announcing the latest Asshole of the Week award winner: In recognition of excellence in assholiness and total indifference to the values of others, the winner is the universally despised senator from Texas: Rafael Edward Cruz.

Although he has a long history of being one of the most despicable individuals ever to hold public office, Rafael's performance, along with future AOTW Josh Hawley, during the confirmation hearings for Judge Ketanji Brown Jackson Cruz attempted to equivalate the accusations against Brett Cavanaugh with a witch hunt, even though nobody had accused Judge Jackson of anything, and injected the absurd concept of "racist babies" while attempting to ridicule critical race theory and the judge. If you witnessed this, you saw a disgusting display of bullying by ineffectual, effeminate men portraying toxic masculinity.

Rafael "Ted" Cruz was born with advantages. As the youngest child, his family was well established and could send him to the finest private schools. His father, Rafael, was an activist against the Fulgencio Batista dictatorship and was beaten for his beliefs. Rafael Cruz was granted political asylum in the United States after attending the University of Texas and became a successful businessman and Canadian citizen. Political courage, or the courage of one's beliefs, is not something that Ted inherited. Ted can show loyalty to someone who calls him "the biggest liar in the world," publicly states his wife is ugly and suggests his father was involved in the assassination of a president if he sees political or monetary gain in it. Watching the debates with Trump was like watching a contest for the greater of two evils.

Ted's political career began contesting election results, so it should be no surprise that he saw the advantage of jumping on "The Big Lie" express. Raffy Ted helped organize the legal team representing Bush in Bush v. Gore only to support overturning an election twenty years later. Apparently, he believes the Republican candidate should be declared the winner regardless of the will of the voters.

His disdain for his constituents was fully displayed when he decided to head for warmer climes while they were freezing. Nothing says "fuck you" like going to Cancun when there is a massive power outage during winter storms. To fully show his innate creepiness, he tried to blame the blackout on wind turbines, which account for less than half the energy than coal and natural gas do in Texas, and then blamed his Cancun gaffe on his daughters. He is most assuredly a scumbag.

Despite his Hispanic heritage, he is a leading advocate of white supremacy. In this regard, he reminds me of a black man hunting escaped slaves. He has opposed numerous bills regarding hate crimes against minorities. He showed a brief moment of sanity when he referred to insurrectionists as terrorists only to cower under pressure from noted racist Tucker Carlson and his racist supporters.

Ted Cruz represents the sole speck of bipartisanship in Congress; members of both parties hate him. To know Ted is to detest Ted. It is hard to decide the most deserving AOTW winner of all time, but I am sure Ted Cruz will be in the running.

Chapter Twenty-one:
Gargantuan Ginni Thomas:
Asshole of the Week

Virginia "Ginni" Thomas was born Virginia Lamb on February 23, 1957. Her birthplace is listed as Omaha, Nebraska, but this is unlikely. Since she is the offspring of a wolverine and an American bison, it is much more likely that she was not born within the city limits. While attending high school in Omaha, she said her ambition was to be elected to Congress, an ambition she abandoned when named an all-conference linebacker in her junior year. Instead, she used her football prowess to obtain an athletic scholarship at Creighton University, where she eventually received a Juris Doctorate.

Her career as an all-star linebacker for the Kansas City Chief was cut short by Chronic Traumatic Encephalopathy, so she moved to Washington to work for Representative Hal Daub. For the four years after leaving the legislative director job with Daub, Ginni worked as an attorney and labor specialist for the U.S. Chamber of Commerce, where she attended congressional hearings and represented business interests. She became an advocate against the Family and Medical Leave Act. Upon leaving the Chamber of Commerce, she worked in the Legislative Affairs Office of the Department of Labor. While there, she argued against equal pay for women in jobs equivalent to men, cementing her legacy as an uncaring rich cunt.

During this period, Ginni married Clarence "Uncle Tom" Thomas, a man who had expressed the desire to marry any white woman who would have him. Luckily for Thomas, Virginia had decided to seize on any opportunity that might enhance her wealth and power.

Ginni's came to fruition when her husband was nominated and confirmed as a Justice of the Supreme Court of the United States. Instead of avoiding possible conflicts of interest by avoiding politics, like spouses of Supreme Court justices have historically done, Ginni jumped in with both feet. She became a policy analyst for House Republican Chairman Dick Armey.

In 2000, Ginni was working for the Heritage Foundation, a conservative "think" tank; the word "think" is loosely used in this context. Her job was to suggest judicial appointments for the George W. Bush administration. Of the two SCOTUS appointments by W., I am confident she was only behind the selection of Samuel "Blabbermouth" Alito. Alito has never met a secret he didn't share.

By 2009, Ginni had established her lobbying group, Liberty Central. The group's stated purpose was to oppose the "leftist tyranny" of President Barack Obama and congressional Democrats. When pressed on the possible conflict of interest posed by her presence at a lobbying firm, she responded with an "everybody's doing it" rationalization. Liberty Central stopped operations in 2012.

Ginni doubled down in 2011 by creating a consulting firm, Liberty Consulting; she was big on liberty but only for the wealthy and influential. The company's website stated that clients could use Thomas' "experience and connections" to help with "governmental affairs efforts" and "political donation strategies" (Vogel, Cogan, and Bresnahan). In her role at Liberty Consulting, she advised political donors on how best to direct funds in the post-citizens *United* climate. That same year she became a correspondent for <em>*The Daily Caller*</em>.

By 2016, Ginni had become a full-time political pundit. She helped found Groundswell with the notorious scumbag Steve Bannon. According to an article by Jonathon Swan in <em>, *Axios*</em>, Thomas urged Trump to change administration personnel and provided him with a list of suggested individuals. In 2019, Virginia became a member of the board of the Council for National Policy, a Christian right-wing group founded during the Reagan administration. In May 2020, Trump appointed her to the trust fund board of The Library of Congress.

Ginni was an election denier and became prominent in the Stop the Steal efforts. She sent emails to legislators in Arizona and Wisconsin urging them to ignore the election results and appoint new slates of electors supportive of Trump. No, not every justice's spouse was doing the things she did.

Whether she is held responsible either criminally or civilly, as well as whether her husband is impeached for aiding her endeavors, remains to be seen. Or she can always roam the plains in search of family members.

SOURCES

Thomas, Ginni. (2022, November 18). In Wikipedia.
    https://en.wikipedia.org/wiki/Ginni_Thomas<li>.
    Vogel, Kenneth P.; Marin Cogan; and John Bresnahan (February 4, 2011). "Justice Thomas' wife
    Virginia Thomas now a lobbyist"
http://www.politico.com/news/stories/0211/48812.html). Politico.

Chapter Twenty-two: Repulsive Ron DeSantis: Asshole of the Week

Our latest winner of the asshole of the week award is Ronald D. DeSantis. Born—perhaps hatched is the more appropriate term—in the cockroach capital of the United States, Jacksonville, Florida, Ronald Dumbass DeSantis was listed as "Cockroach" under "race" on his birth certificate. His parents were unknown as there were so many candidates. RDD spent most of his childhood in Dunedin—named after the rangers in Tolkien's *The Lord of the Rings*—FL.

After attending a Catholic school, Ron the Repulsive, as he came to be known by his "friends," graduated from Dunedin High School—home of the "Fighting Cow Pies"—in 1997. Yale University lacked cockroaches, so via affirmative action, he was admitted. The repulsive one studied history at Yale and graduated *magma cum loudly* in 2001. After a year of teaching history to entitled teens at a private school in Georgia, Ronald decided to apply to Harvard and was admitted for many of the same reasons. He graduated *cum loudly* with a Juris Doctor degree in 2005.

During his second year at Harvard, he was commissioned to the Navy JAG Corps as a lieutenant junior grade and began work as a Navy prosecutor in 2005. Because of his commitment to "guilty until proven innocent," he was promoted to lieutenant. Ron was deployed to Iraq in 2007, where he spent most of his time cowering and attempting to hide behind the more significant members of Seal Team One. As of this date, he is still in the Navy Reserve, although it is rumored that he has hired a lookalike in case of emergency.

Ron decided by 2012 that he had run out of jobs where you get paid for doing nothing and decided to run for Congress. With voters in Florida's 6th District aching for the repulsive, he was reelected in 2014 and 2016. Some of Ron's more memorable legislative acts include introducing a bill that would have required the DOJ to Congress any time they thought an executive agency was failing to enforce a law or regulation, presumedly including those regulations the agency had enacted; signing a pledge to vote against any climate change legislation; adding a rider to a spending bill that would have ended funding for the Mueller investigation; and generally being a douchebag.

Repulsive Ron decided to run for Governor of Florida to succeed Rick Scott and ensure the legacy of douchebag governors continued. Ron firmly attached his lips to Donald Trump's ass, causing some to say it resembled a sea lamprey attached to a lake trout. Putting any sense of decency aside, DeSantis decided to exploit his family in the campaign. He demonstrated his loyalty to Trump by running ads that featured him showing his children how to build a wall and having a daughter dressed in a red jumper that said: "Make America Great Again." Unfortunately, child abuse charges were never filed.

It is as governor that the repulsive one finally was able to put his full douchebaggery on display. His platform included his support for legislation allowing those with concealed weapons permits to quit hiding them. He supported a law banning sanctuary cities from protecting undocumented immigrants. He endorsed a state constitutional amendment requiring a supermajority for any tax increase. His opposition to Medicaid for able-bodied adults without children. He either believes there are no working people who are poor or doesn't give a shit.

During his stint as governor, he became even more repulsive: He attempted to put all the blame on Sheriff Scott Israel by firing him for his department's response after the shooting at the Fort Lauderdale airport and Marjory Stoneman Douglas High School. He appointed three knee-jerk conservative judges as replacements for vacancies, thereby switching the Florida Supreme Court majority from liberal to conservative, during his first two weeks in office. Even though he said, during his campaign, that education decisions should be made locally, he signed an executive order ending Common Core in Florida. He signed legislation that would make it harder for ballot initiatives to be successful. There were petition gathering works underway for legalizing medical marijuana, increasing the minimum wage, and expanding Medicaid. He could not tolerate legislation that would help the poor and disadvantaged.

Also, as governor, he supported the big lie. Since it is hard to imagine someone who graduated from two Ivy League schools could be stupid enough to believe blatant nonsense, he had to be incredibly gullible or feigning belief for political reasons.

Repulsive Ron also drafted legislation protecting Confederate monuments, undermining efforts by local authorities to regulate their police forces and blocking people injured while protesting from receiving damages.

Ron and his RWNJ legislators have passed some of the most draconian voter restriction laws in the counting. If nothing else, this alone would have qualified him for AOTW infamy.

Chapter Twenty-three:
Kanye "Crazy Ye" West:
Asshole of the Week

Kanye—he prefers "Ye" because two syllables are just too hard—was born sometime in 1977. Little else about his birth is certain. According to the original account, he was found in a basket floating down a gutter on a flooded street in Atlanta and stopped by reeds from an overgrown lawn. Once he found out that Moses was Jewish, the story changed to a barn in a rural area between Atlanta and Conroy. He is sticking with this account since no one has yet to inform him that Jesus was also a reformist Jew.

Kanye was raised in an upper-middle-class environment in Oak Lawn, Illinois, until he was ten. He moved with his mother to Nanjing, China, where his mother taught at the university. It was there that someone informed him that he was black, an account he refuses to acknowledge to this day. According to his mother, he attended school there and picked up the language quickly. Does it seem somewhat strange that he forgot nearly all of it, or is it just me? When asked about his grades, he said, "I got A's and B's"—although "诶'艾丝" and "比'艾丝" might be more accurate.

Kanye attended the American Academy of Art and later Chicago State University but dropped out at the age of twenty to pursue a musical career. He acknowledges the great wisdom of this decision by creating a music album called "College Dropout." I am not going to go into any detail about his musical career since, until today, I have no recollection of ever. I listened to something called "Golddigger" today, which was enough for me. Call me an old-fashioned rock boomer, but I think good music involves more than rhyming lyrics, a heavy bass line, and percussion. Kanye chose to call his music studio "Donda" but swears that two syllables are his absolute limit.

Kayne seems to have a fetish for very large asses because he married Kim Kardashian. The Kardashians are a family that became famous by being famous. It must have something to do with their deceased father and OJ lawyer combined with a consumer fervor for inane reality shows. Why anyone would want to keep up with the Kardashians is beyond my comprehension. These shows are accurate and well acted as a Shakespeare's play performance by third-grade students.

There are two significant traits you should know about Kanye. He is not one to knock softly and politely enter and does not work and play well with others. The list of other musicians of his era that he either crashed their performances or insulted in the press is too long to detail here. He is the paradigm of loud-mouthed assholes.

It wasn't until his embrace of evangelical Christianity that he became "elevator does go to the top floor, toys in the attic, batshit" crazy. For some reason, like other evangelical Christians, they chose to endorse Donald Trump as some divine messenger—this is the moral equivalent of viewing Adolph Hitler as an ambassador of democracy. But, like most preferences of the Christian right, it is impossible to link them to any teaching in the New Testament.

The fallout from his deranged ideas and behavior has only recently dropped. His antisemitic rants have caused him to lose his contract with Adidas and several retail outlets. Kanye has never been reluctant to follow up crazy with demented. His response to the Adidas decision was to march into Skechers headquarters and demand to negotiate a new contract, without realizing that his "Jew-controlled business world" extended to Skechers management and significant shareholders. He was ceremoniously escorted from the premises and told never to return.

If there is one way to spot an asshole worthy of recognition, it is the lack of sympathy for his misfortunes. Kanye has few who feel badly for how the ravens have come home to roost; the general reaction has been humor and glee. This guy's asshole award has been a long time coming.

Chapter Twenty-four: Marco Rubio: Asshole of the Week

Marco Rubio was born without a spine on the day I graduated high school. Luckily, he was born in Miami, where a crack medical supplied him with a synthetic spine made of stale marshmallows from the previous Halloween. He must undergo replacement surgery yearly on the same date to ensure the marshmallows are stiff enough to support his tiny frame. The procedures are successful, but he has been cautioned to avoid campfires, chocolate, and graham crackers.

Marco's parents were Cubans who were deported to the United States by the Batista for running a bunko operation involving knock-off cigars and diluted rum—water from El Lago is added and rebottled. Marco seems to suffer from bouts of confusion on the date his parents left Cuba. I am sure it is just an honest mistake, and the three-year difference has nothing to do with the fact that leaving after Castro took control is considered a political asset in the South Florida Cuban community. In contrast, those who left in the Batista years are viewed with suspicion.

Marco was a slight child and suffered bullying in school. When it was discovered that his spine gave his body a unique percussion rebound quality, he became a substitute in soccer games in the poorer areas of Miami, where the children could not afford a ball. He still holds the Miami school system record for both goals scored and saves.

The Rubios were devout Catholics and only began to attend the Mormon church after they moved to Nevada because they had come to believe that Native Americans really were the lost tribes of Israel and that Jesus was from the Brooklyn area.

Mario later returned to Florida and was confirmed as a Catholic because he remembered he was from Miami, not Salt Lake City. After graduating from a Miami area high school, he was offered a music scholarship at a small college in Missouri.

Mario was an accomplished skin flutist, a talent that would come in handy during the Trump years. He attended a community college in Miami, got a bachelor of arts degree from the University of Florida and a Juris Doctorate from the University of Miami (or the other way around, who gives a shit?).

Marco made almost no impression on his law school classmates. During his disastrous presidential primary run in 2016, the *University of Miami* newspaper sought quotes from fellow alumni. The following are quotes: "I remember he was well spoken," said one classmate, who couldn't recall any personal interactions. "Oh, that guy… I think I remember that guy," said another. Another classmate who had met with Rubio on several occasions could only comment that he was focused on academics and "he was quite taken with politics, as I recall…." These are not the sort of comments made about a leader.

Realizing he was never going to be a successful or competent attorney, Marco focused on politics early on. Two years after finishing law school, he became the city commissioner of West Miami. In a safe Republican district, he won the primary runoff by 64 votes and became a Florida House of Representatives member. Since they only work sixty days a year, Marco languished here for the next nine years. As a reward for his work on the gerrymandering committee, he was named the first Cuban American speaker of the Florida House of Representatives.

During his time as a Florida legislator, Marco was deemed a moderate who could work with the other party. It wasn't until he reached the U.S. Senate that he went into full-asshole mode. In 2010 he was elected to the U.S. Senate after defeating then-Republican Charlie Crist and a Democratic opponent.

Many will remember his thirsty response to the State of the Union address in 2013 as the time when he officially became a buffoon. During his tenure in the Senate, he voted against background checks for purchasing guns, opposed the publication of the CIA's "enhanced interrogation techniques," worked to gut the Affordable Care Act, defended Trump's rescindment of DACA, opposed the nomination of Merrick Garland to the SCOTUS because it was the last year in a presidential term but supported the nomination of Amy Barrett Comey under the same conditions.

After calling Trump a "con artist," "…wholly unprepared to be president of the United States," and noted that the country should not hand "the nuclear codes of the United States to an erratic individual," after Trump's election, Mario had a complete change of heart and supported the most outrageous policies. One could imagine that he employed his skin flutist talents and he and Trump became connected at the lips.

Chapter Twenty-five:
Mitch "Mr. Malicious" McConnell:
Asshole of the Week

Addison Mitchell McConnell III was born to a pair of terrapins in an Alabama bayou on, as far as we can tell—they didn't keep good records on the births of turtles—February 20, 1942. The media is not as concerned with the age of the Senate minority leader—a position in which he will remain until he retires or is defeated—as they are the age of the president. Upon judging his son's demeanor, Addison Jr. bought a funeral home, thinking his son's natural dour appearance would make him a natural funeral director.

Mitch III, hereafter I will refer to him as Mitch, contracted polio at the age of two. The treatment saved him from permanent disability and nearly bankrupted the family. After Jr. did a stint in the army at Fort Gordon, the family moved to Louisville. Mitch attended high school there and shattered his father's dreams by choosing political science instead of mortuary science. While attending the University of Louisville, Mitch tried out for the football and basketball teams. He did not make either team, and both coaches voiced the same evaluation: "He just won't stick his neck out."

Mitch graduated from UofL with a B.A. in Political Science and a minor in Knowing and Screwing Enemies. He received his law degree from the University of Kentucky School of Law in 1967. His educational deferment expired upon his graduation, and the Vietnam War was reaching its peak. Rather than take that risk, Mitch joined the Army Reserve as a private. His first day was two days after taking the bar exam. He served 37 days before being diagnosed with rare optic neuritis and was classified as medically unfit for service.

With his military service and the prospect of going to Vietnam out of the way, Mitch decided to pursue his dream of being America's Greatest Asshole full-time (this was the reason behind his uneasy relationship with Donald Trump, whom he viewed as a rival for the award). From 1968 to 1970, Mitch served as the chief legislative assistant to Kentucky Senator Marlow Cook, whom he later declared his mentor.

He volunteered for an unsuccessful gubernatorial race and attempted to run for the state legislature but did not meet the residential requirements. He then spent the next three years working for a Louisville law firm. From 1974 – 1976 Mitch worked in the Attorney General's office of the Ford administration. While there, he worked with and was influenced by Robert Bork and Antonin Scalia.

His political career began in 1977, when he was elected to the top office of Jefferson County judge/executive. He was reelected in 1981, when he outspent his Democratic opponent 3 to 1, a tactic he would employ for the remainder of his career. Mitch was elected to the Senate in 1984 and has held that position. He was initially described as a pragmatist and moderate Republican known to support abortion rights and public unions. He later discovered that the route to power in the Republican party involved becoming a right-wing douchebag, a philosophy he came to embrace fully.

Mitch served as chairman of the National Republican Senatorial Committee and voted to convict and remove President Bill Clinton from office in 1999. Lying about a blow job was a much more grievous offense than all the crap that Trump pulled in four years. Later he became Majority Whip. In 2006, Bill Frist chose to step down as Majority Leader. After losing in November, Mitch was elected Minority Leader. With the filibuster, he now had the power to abuse, and abuse it he did. University of Texas legal scholar noted that after Mitch observed how Democratic cooperation helped Bush get reelected in 2004, "McConnell altogether … rationally concluded that Republicans have nothing to gain, as a political party, from collaborating with anything that the president could then claim as an achievement." Mitch had gone from caring about the welfare of his constituents to a full-blown obstructionist.

Mitch did everything he could to delay the enactment of or defeat popular programs like healthcare, financial reform, and economic stimulus. The Republican caucus repeatedly threatened to allow the United States to default on its debts. McConnell once stated that he had learned from the 2011 debt-ceiling crisis that "it's a hostage worth ransoming." The icing on the obstructionist's cake was denying President Obama's appointment of Merrick Garland to the Supreme Court and ensuring that the Court would be filled with right-wing morons who would later overturn Roe v. Wade.

By the time of Trump's election, Mitch was only concerned with political power and personal wealth. In 2018, McConnell was named by Open Secrets as the wealthiest member of the Senate, with an estimated wealth of $25 million. That number doubled after the death of his mother-in-law.

He twice voted not to convict Trump in impeachment trials for offenses far more heinous than hiding a blow job. He even declared Trump guilty after his second vote to not condemn. Despite rare expressions of support for democracy and the Constitution, it has become apparent that Addison III has earned his recognition of assholedom.